Unders

MW00577545

Jo Cooke is Director of Hoa
decluttering and an accredited member or the Association
Declutterers and Organizers (APDO). She has been running her own
business, Tapioca Tidy, since 2013. Jo previously had a varied career in char-
itable organizations, human resources, project management, book-keeping
and the civil service, but realized that she had a flair for decluttering and
organizing when she had to sell the family home that her father had
lived in for more than 30 years. She has a wealth of the experience and
skills required when working with hoarders and takes a responsible and
empathetic approach to the needs of people from both areas of her work,
clutterbugs and hoarders.

Overcoming Common Problems Series

Selected titles

A full list of titles is available from Sheldon Press,
36 Causton Street, London SW1P 4ST and on our website at
www.sheldonpress.co.uk

Beating Insomnia: Without really trying
Dr Tim Cantopher

Chronic Fatigue Syndrome: What you need to know about CFS/ME
Dr Megan A. Arroll

Cider Vinegar
Margaret Hills

Coeliac Disease: What you need to know
Alex Gazzola

Coping Successfully with Hiatus Hernia
Dr Tom Smith

Coping with a Mental Health Crisis: Seven steps to healing
Catherine G. Lucas

Coping with Difficult Families
Dr Jane McGregor and Tim McGregor

Coping with Endometriosis
Jill Eckersley and Dr Zara Aziz

Coping with Memory Problems
Dr Sallie Baxendale

Coping with Schizophrenia
Professor Kevin Gournay and Debbie Robson

Coping with the Psychological Effects of Illness
Dr Fran Smith, Dr Carina Eriksen and Professor Robert Bor

Coping with Thyroid Disease
Mark Greener

Depression and Anxiety the Drug-Free Way
Mark Greener

Depressive Illness: The curse of the strong
Dr Tim Cantopher

Dr Dawn's Guide to Brain Health
Dr Dawn Harper

Dr Dawn's Guide to Digestive Health
Dr Dawn Harper

Dr Dawn's Guide to Healthy Eating for Diabetes
Dr Dawn Harper

Dr Dawn's Guide to Healthy Eating for IBS
Dr Dawn Harper

Dr Dawn's Guide to Heart Health
Dr Dawn Harper

Dr Dawn's Guide to Sexual Health
Dr Dawn Harper

Dr Dawn's Guide to Weight and Diabetes
Dr Dawn Harper

Dr Dawn's Guide to Women's Health
Dr Dawn Harper

The Fibromyalgia Healing Diet
Christine Craggs-Hinton

Helping Elderly Relatives
Jill Eckersley

How to Stop Worrying
Dr Frank Tallis

Invisible Illness: Coping with misunderstood conditions
Dr Megan A. Arroll and Professor Christine P. Dancey

Living with Fibromyalgia
Christine Craggs-Hinton

Living with Hearing Loss
Dr Don McFerran, Lucy Handscomb and Dr Cherilee Rutherford

Living with the Challenges of Dementia: A guide for family and friends
Patrick McCurry

Overcoming Emotional Abuse: Survive and heal
Susan Elliot-Wright

Overcoming Low Self-esteem with Mindfulness
Deborah Ward

Overcoming Worry and Anxiety
Dr Jerry Kennard

Post-Traumatic Stress Disorder: Recovery after accident and disaster
Professor Kevin Gournay

The Stroke Survival Guide
Mark Greener

Ten Steps to Positive Living
Dr Windy Dryden

Treating Arthritis: The drug-free way
Margaret Hills and Christine Horner

Understanding High Blood Pressure
Dr Shahid Aziz and Dr Zara Aziz

Understanding Yourself and Others: Practical ideas from the world of coaching
Bob Thomson

When Someone You Love Has Dementia
Susan Elliot-Wright

The Whole Person Recovery Handbook
Emma Drew

Overcoming Common Problems

Understanding Hoarding

JO COOKE

sheldon PRESS

First published in Great Britain in 2017

Sheldon Press
36 Causton Street
London SW1P 4ST
www.sheldonpress.co.uk

Copyright © Jo Cooke 2017

All rights reserved. No part of this book may be reproduced or
transmitted in any form or by any means, electronic or mechanical,
including photocopying, recording, or by any information storage and
retrieval system, without permission in writing from the publisher.

The author and publisher have made every effort to ensure that the
external website and email addresses included in this book are correct and
up to date at the time of going to press. The author and publisher are not
responsible for the content, quality or continuing accessibility of the sites.

British Library Cataloguing-in-Publication Data
A catalogue record for this book is available from the British Library

ISBN 978-1-84709-453-7
eBook ISBN 978-1-84709-454-4

Typeset by Fakenham Prepress Solutions, Fakenham, Norfolk NR21 8NN
First printed in Great Britain by Ashford Colour Press
Subsequently digitally reprinted in Great Britain

eBook by Fakenham Prepress Solutions, Fakenham, Norfolk NR21 8NN

Produced on paper from sustainable forests

For people who hoard

Contents

Acknowledgements

I would like to acknowledge my true appreciation of all those who have contributed to this book. In no particular order, thanks are due to Amanda Peet for her role as former Director of Hoarding Disorders UK, for her passion and also for her contribution to the section relating to Emotional Freedom Technique in Chapter 8.

Thanks to Cherry Rudge for her wonderful contributions on ADHD and perfectionism, for the diagram on ADHD and for sharing the story of her client, Peter.

Thanks to Heather Matuozzo for K's story and for her sound advice when I have needed guidance, and to Lynn Howells for her openness, honesty and support, not only with her contribution to the book but also her commitment to our support group in Bracknell.

I would also like to thank all the people I have spoken with and met who have been impacted by 'stuff' for their stories and contributions. Their input has been invaluable in writing this book.

Note: for people who hoard, their families and friends

It's important to be sensitive in our use of language when talking about hoarding, and we need to use terminology that respects individuals' dignity and avoids labelling them. 'A Psychological Perspective on Hoarding', a division of the Clinical Psychology Good Practice Guidelines published by the British Psychological Society, uses the term 'people with hoarding difficulties'. One of the people we work with prefers the term 'clutteree'! However, when referring to someone who hoards, for the sake of brevity and clarity I have also respectfully used 'hoarder', a term which is in common usage and person-centred.

Certain names have been changed to protect the identity of the individuals whose stories and contributions have been included in this book.

Introduction

For centuries, as a result of deprivation and scarcity, both humans and animals have hoarded and accumulated not only foodstuffs but also objects. Just as squirrels hoard nuts to feed themselves through the winter months, and magpies collect objects for their nests, so do humans preserve and stockpile foods, water and other essentials to see them through periods of shortage, recessions, war or natural disaster. Many of us, too, were brought up by parents and grandparents who were wartime babies, and who consequently hoarded to see them through periods of rationing and austerity. Historically we have hoarded as a natural response to being unable to gain easy access to certain foods and essentials, or to being 'stuck inside' during bad weather. We stack and stock logs, tins of food, coffee, nappies, toiletries and medicines. There are generations of 'just in case' hoarders, hateful of waste and fearful of running out. Observe food shoppers panic buying just before bank holidays, at Easter and Christmas – loaves of bread and bags of potatoes fly off the shelves.

Nowadays we so easily and readily dispose of many items, abandoning clothes that are no longer in fashion, books we have read, household and technological items that are no longer cutting-edge, toys that our children have outgrown. With the ever-increasing urge to purge, and a growing culture of decluttering, there is a new throwaway generation. Items can be so easily bought and accessed: shops are open on Sundays, while buying online is easy and readily accessible. If we need a new winter coat, we don't wait until Christmas, we can buy it here and now, at midnight, on our phone or our computer, and receive it in three or four days, or even pay extra for next-day delivery. We have throwaway plates, disposable napkins, pre-chopped garlic, pre-peeled oranges, prefab houses, and electrical items that are not designed to be fixed or repaired. Invariably, as our washing machine, TV or dishwasher becomes faulty, we tend to replace it, not repair it.

Buy one, get one free – who can resist such a bargain offer? Shops in every high street sell products for a pound, charity shops are popping up everywhere – 50p an item. There are car boot and jumble sales every weekend. Stuff is readily accessible everywhere, and shopping and buying is steadily becoming a recreation, a social event. No wonder our homes, garages and sheds are crammed full.

In more recent times, it has been recognized that the reasons for hoarding are not just deprivation and the need to survive disaster, but are far broader, more complex. It is now widely acknowledged that hoarding can be linked to deep-seated psychological and emotional issues. We hoard as a way of seeking comfort and distraction from trauma and difficult life events, and hoarding is often connected with other mental health issues. Hoarding is a solution to a problem and can act as a comfort blanket, just as people may drink, gamble, exercise excessively or over-eat as a coping mechanism.

Possessions play an important part in people's lives. They can define who we are as individuals, and provide us with pleasure, comfort, joy, convenience and opportunity. But accumulating possessions that impact adversely on our living spaces, put a strain on our finances, affect our physical and mental health, and challenge our relationships and our homes can cause significant distress. Hoarding can greatly affect a person's ability to function and carries a high level of risk to those who hoard, the people they are living with and others. Excessive acquiring and saving, collecting items others have thrown away, and not throwing anything away ourselves, can all qualify as characteristics of hoarding.

Hoarding is being increasingly recognized as a mental health disorder. The media has done much to bring hoarding into the limelight, but the subject is frequently portrayed in sensational terms. When the British Psychological Society (BPS) issued a perspective on hoarding, one of its recommendations was that 'The national media should seek advice from experts including clinical psychologists about the portrayal of people with hoarding problems and desist from using mental health problems to entertain and shock the public.'

This book is designed to help those who are affected by hoarding difficulties, including friends and family members. I hope it will raise awareness and provide not only a better understanding of and insight into hoarding, but also tools and techniques for those wanting to help. I hope too to help reduce the stigma surrounding hoarding. Language used by the media, the portrayal of hoarders' homes, and drastic means of 'helping', such as insisting on a dramatic clearout, have all been damaging. It is not always possible, shoppers are easily spotted at car boot sales and in charity shops, and demonstrate a sense of urgency and thirst in purchasing their goods.

Physical implications

People who hoard severely are likely to have difficulty in caring for themselves physically and are at risk of neglecting their health needs. Any existing medical conditions they have may well be exacerbated by the insanitary conditions in which they live and by their limited access to washing and cleaning facilities. Lung conditions, respiratory problems and asthma are prevalent among people living in hoarded homes. Skin conditions can also arise. I myself once caught scabies through working in a hoarded home that had become infested with fleas.

We should also be mindful that if someone in a hoarded home is taken ill, emergency services and ambulance personnel may well face daunting restrictions in being able to access the patient, whose health may become further compromised by such difficulties.

Some homes become infested with rats. As a result, the rats' urine and faeces may become trapped with the person's belongings; over time ammonia will be released into the air, causing breathing difficulties. Additionally there is the danger of contracting Weil's disease, or leptospirosis, a bacterial infection caused by contact with infected animals, with their urine or blood, or with contaminated water or soil. Officially rare in the UK, and usually a hazard for livestock workers, in the majority of cases leptospirosis causes mild flu-like symptoms, such as a headache, chills and muscle pain, but in some cases infection can be more severe. If you suspect you have contracted leptospirosis, do visit your GP, who can prescribe antibiotics.

There are also clearly the risks of slips, trips and hazards caused by a cluttered home. We often talk about minimizing the risk of avalanches. Many people I know will tell me that they are woken in the night by the sound of a pile that has collapsed and caused an avalanche of hoarded items.

Self-neglect

Chapter 14 of the Care Act 2014 Statutory Guidance recognizes self-neglect as a type of abuse. The description of self-neglect encompasses a wide range of behaviours but broadly entails neglecting to care for one's personal hygiene, health or surroundings, and includes behaviour such as hoarding. Self-neglect may include situations where an individual is unable to access hot water, a sink or facilities for washing clothes.

In extreme cases, people in this situation have been diagnosed with Diogenes syndrome, which essentially involves living in squalor and exhibiting not only a marked indifference to one's living conditions and personal hygiene, but social isolation, refusal of help, and a failure to seek or to follow medical advice. In my experience, some hoarders have been misdiagnosed with Diogenes syndrome – perhaps because, given the lack of clarity among local councils in regard to helping hoarders, it provides an easy label for some people to access the help and support they need from social services and environmental health.

Types of hoarded items

Although the items that hoarders are emotionally attached to vary, there are areas of clutter that are common and can be grouped as follows:

- paper clutter
- electronic clutter
- food
- storage containers
- sentimental items
- books
- digital items
- clothes
- tools

Paper and newspapers

Paper is one of the items that hoarders most commonly keep. What is written on the paper, and the form in which it is collected, varies from suitcases of old to-do lists, shopping lists, Christmas card lists, birthday cards or postcards to newspapers, junk mail, pizza delivery menus, unopened bills, letters, newsletters, magazines and books.

When I gave a talk to a Women's Institute group on hoarding, many of the women in the audience could relate to the hoarding of newspapers and knew family members and friends who hoarded newspapers neatly stacked in piles on shelves, in garages and coal sheds, or under chairs – some tied with string and some contained in boxes or old kitchen sinks and stored in lofts.

I have met many people with a love of newspapers, and many of our hoarding support group members have challenges with newspapers. They retain them for an array of reasons. They are a way of hoarding information, and many of my clients feel they have to read and flick through each newspaper before recycling it. Newspapers act as a form of history, as a timeline for the person's life, and as a representation of local life – which people somehow feel part of by keeping the newspaper.

I worked with a lady who had a tea-chest of mementos of significant events that had happened during her lifetime. It included extracts from newspapers detailing the events of 9/11, the divorce of Prince Charles and Diana, the UK floods in 2008, all the details of obituaries and notifications of the deaths and births of people she knew. These articles and cuttings represented her timeline and her presence in the world, and formed an important part of her identity.

Magazines

Magazines present dreams, hopes, aspirations and an ever-flowing invitation to escape from reality. They also provide information, history, intelligence, crosswords and recipes. I worked with one person who kept each Sunday newspaper magazine on the basis that she wanted to keep the recipes and any tips on dieting. She did not know how to cook and her kitchen was too cluttered to access the oven, so that she tended to live off microwaveable ready-made meals. But she aspired to learn to cook and to lose weight, and she saw the magazines as representing her dreams. We use the term 'aspirational clutter' for the hoarding of things that we will never use, never read, never wear.

Junk mail

Junk mail is another allurement – everything from new furniture to spring bulbs and new pizza toppings. Many of us don't have time to look at it, and may promptly recycle it, but some people hang on to it as another representation of their dreams and goals, or perhaps through the fear of missing something that might add to the quality of their lives. The Royal Mail offer an opt-out from junk mail. It is a free service that will stop unsolicited, unaddressed mail being delivered. Signing up to the scheme is the single most effective measure you can take to reduce junk mail.

One problem can be squirrelling junk mail away until it has been read before discarding it, which may reach extreme lengths in some people with hoarding difficulties. One social worker spoke to me of her frustration with a client who had agreed to her junk mail being recycled. The social worker returned the following week to discover that the woman had retrieved all the junk mail from the recycling bin. It transpired that the process of removing it all in one session was too rushed, and that she needed to look at it before recycling it. Rules were made, and when the social worker returned again, it was established that any food takeaway menus and certain telephone and television leaflets could be automatically recycled, but that she wanted to look at the rest first.

Books

Who doesn't love books? I was mortified when my home was flooded and the collection of orange Penguin books that I had enjoyed reading as a teenager was ruined. We can have a complex relationship with books. We read to escape; we buy to enjoy, to acquire knowledge and new findings, and we also buy with a view that our books represent who we want to be, how we want to be perceived; they form part of our identity as someone who is appreciative of art, an intellectual, a politician, an aspiring philosopher.

Some of the individuals I work with are avid collectors of books – they may have a thirst for knowledge, or need to acquire every new updated edition of dictionaries. *Tsundoku* (literally 'reading pile') is a Japanese noun that describes a person who buys books but doesn't read them, and lets them pile up in the hallway, on the floor, on bookshelves and furniture.

Bibliomania can be a facet of obsessive–compulsive disorder when it involves the collecting or hoarding of books to the point where social relations or health are damaged. Books may be purchased in multiple copies. Some are read, others are preserved in their bags. Some people have been convicted of stealing books, and a few may have even committed murder through their passion for books.

Yoghurt pots and plastic containers

Food storage items are a surprisingly common form of clutter. Who doesn't have extra plastic containers stored in a cupboard 'just in case', perhaps to store food for freezing, or for other domestic uses? I think there must be a heaven for plastic lids and odd socks, and we know many people who reuse plastic containers which have previously contained food items such as taramasalata, salad dressing, grapes, peaches and so on. It seems that keeping and accumulating such storage boxes makes some people feel organized and in control.

A few people with hoarding difficulties feel somewhat challenged by their collection of containers and agonize over whether a container should be disposed of, dwelling at length on how it might be of use within their home. Thankfully, certain plastics can be recycled.

One support worker told the story of how he was helping someone clear up their kitchen, and without asking or consulting the individual, he took it upon himself to deem the yoghurt pots rubbish. When the person learned that his yoghurt pots had been thrown away into black bin bags, he literally tore each bag open and retrieved them all. In addition to being valuable to him for their shape, the pots to him were useful for housing nails, paper clips, stamps and other important items. It is important to recognize that although you think an item valueless, the opinion of the person you are wanting to help may well differ.

I worked with one woman who was unhappy about reducing her assortment of plastic containers (she lived alone and had over 50 of them) until she had found the accompanying lids. There was simply no room to spread them out to try and match lid to container unless we took them out into the garden. We decided to revisit her stock in the summer, and when she reviewed her containers she was happy not to go through the challenge of matching them up again and was relieved to let them go. The passage of time and the revisiting of earlier decisions has a way of determining the destination of our things.

Animal hoarding

The tragedy of animal hoarding is that not only can the lives of the animals involved be severely compromised, but also those of the animal hoarders themselves, as a result of poor sanitation and the risk of disease. Quite often the hoarder is unable to understand and recognize that the animals are at risk, and incapable of providing an adequate level of care.

How do you illustrate the difference between collecting, breeding and/or hoarding animals? The Hoarding of Animals Research Consortium (HARC) gives the following criteria for identifying the hoarding of animals:

- having more than the typical number of companion animals;
- failure to provide even minimal standards of nutrition, sanitation, shelter and veterinary care, the neglect often resulting in the illness and death from starvation of the animals, the spread of infectious disease, and untreated injuries or medical conditions;
- the person's denial of his or her inability to provide minimum standards of care and the impact of that failure on the animals, the household, and the human occupants of the dwelling;
- persistence, despite this failure, in accumulating and controlling animals.

Why do people hoard animals? As with the hoarding of objects, the reasons and triggers for animal hoarding can be complex, and are often associated with childhood trauma and neglect. One lady we worked with, Diane, felt that her hoard of cats provided her with a relationship free of conflict and complications – a reassurance of unconditional love. She had not had a good relationship with her own mother, who had denied her toys and love and had constantly reminded her that she wished she had been born a boy. Diane treated her cats as her babies, bought them toys and talked to them constantly. Her cats acted as a substitute for the loving relationships she had not been able to form on a human level. She sought solace in her cats' love for and dependency on her and became blind to and overwhelmed by the deplorable conditions in which both she and the cats were living.

We took away over 20 cats from her home, and on each visit she mourned and did not feel able to come with us to Cats Protection. We had however visited the agency before considering asking her to let go of her cats, so at least she knew where they were going and that they would be looked after. We worked closely with the various agencies involved: RSPCA, vets, Cats Protection, social services and environmental health. A multi-agency approach is key to helping an animal hoarder.

Again – as when dealing with the hoarding of objects – we did not take the cats from the house in one go but over the course of three visits in the space of a few months. To take them all at once would have been too traumatic, and Cats Protection would hardly have been able to house them all. A few months on we were pleased to learn that some of the cats had been found new homes on the condition that they were rehomed in pairs. The cats had been accustomed to living closely together in the hoarded home, so it would have been traumatic to rehome them singly.

Digital hoarding

It is easy to replace one form of activity with another, and the same can go for clutter. In some cases, I know people who have replaced physical clutter with digital clutter. This activity can absorb just as much time, money and resource as the physical stuff.

We have access to electronic information from the internet 24 hours a day and the temptation of information to download, photos to scan, PDF documents to save, then leads to needing more online storage. Many people hoard information – and now there is also a way of storing it digitally. This often leads to difficulties; with so much on it, the overloaded computer slows down or fails to function as it should. More computers, laptops, iPads and further 'electronic space' are purchased. The same applies to mobile phones. With new applications being made constantly available – for maps, restaurants, online banking, diets, and so on – phones slow down and some people are unable to use their phone for its intended purpose because of the sheer amount of information stored.

Homeless hoarding

You may wonder how hoarding and homelessness connect, and if there is a correlation between the two. As a matter of fact, we have had several enquiries from workers supporting the homeless in hostels and shelters who want to gain a better understanding of why some of their clients hoard.

Take the story of a woman called Sonia, who lives in New York. Sonia is a Puerto Rican who has been married twice and apparently lost her four-year-old twin boys in a car accident. Sonia has been homeless and hoarding for many years, and is known to the locals as 'Choo Choo' because of the train of shopping trolleys she has built up. It has been reported that recently police officers and sanitation workers threw nearly all of Sonia's 'stuff' away and tried to convince her to seek help at a homeless shelter. She had over 20 shopping trolleys that she moved around the city – some containing newspapers, plastic bottles and cardboard and others her clothes. After the police had removed most of Sonia's 'home', she quickly built it up again by filling up two laundry carts the next day. She insists that she feels safer living on the streets and that her shopping trolleys act as protection for her. She puts sticks in between the wheels of the trolleys, both to stop them rolling away and to prevent other people from taking them.

Our homes act as our nests, as our havens and places of sanctuary. The homeless too need to feel safe and, without the fallback of a home, some homeless people strive to create a sense of safety, security and control through hoarding. Hoarding provides insulation and acts as a life raft. Their hoard gives them a portable nest and alleviates the fear they feel for their future: 'No stuff = not safe'. The homeless hoard through fear of losing again all that they have, as a connection to a past that might have been prosperous, and an investment against the fear of the future and the uncertainly and fear of what that might hold.

Compulsive acquiring

People who hoard find it difficult to stop themselves acquiring things. They buy and gather far more than they need, from free newspapers at railway stations or free samples in shops, to tomato ketchup sachets, sugar sachets, napkins, even rubber bands off the pavement. One lady I know finds it difficult to pass apple trees, blackberry bushes and chestnuts without feeling the urge to gather some and bring them home. Bargain buying too is difficult for a hoarder to resist. The acquiring acts as retail therapy, producing a feeling of warmth as soon as the person has bought the object.

Perfectionism

Hoarders tend to be perfectionists with poor decision-making abilities. Given the uncertainties of life and the things that can go wrong, it's not surprising that some people feel the need to strive for perfection with the things they can control.

In an article for *Autism Asperger's Digest* in 2010, Temple Grandin (the world-renowned autism spokesperson) writes that in the case of autism and Asperger syndrome, it's apparently not uncommon for affected individuals to tend towards black and white thinking – they see themselves and the world around them in polar opposites, which feeds their need to be perfect. Cherry Rudge, the daughter of a hoarder, recalls that 'My mum and I would often look at each other and shake our heads in disbelief whenever Dad categorically contradicted or disagreed with something that was factually entirely correct – in effect calling black white.' Grandin says of such people in her article, 'Even the tiniest mistakes and mishaps can feel like monumental failures to them, creating high levels of anxiety when their efforts or the events around them do not measure up to this all-or-nothing scale.'

Cherry Rudge agrees: 'Again, it seemed to me that nothing I ever did was good enough for my dad, and he attempted to control my life even into adulthood. I don't remember him praising me for anything I'd done, or showing any affection, until the later stages of his life.'

So perfectionism – irrespective of the state of someone's physical or mental health – may go some way to explaining why people affected by clutter, disorganization or hoarding can head in one or more of various directions, including:

- becoming like rabbits caught in headlights when presented with problems – they may not know how to approach the problem perfectly, so they do little or nothing about it;
- rushing at things without getting anywhere;
- hyper-focus on working on just one thing, to make it as perfect as they can – often to the exclusion of higher priorities, often including relationships;
- becoming compulsive completists, not satisfied until they have everything to complete a set;
- only focusing on the things that attract their attention, or make them feel good or rewarded, as those things are less daunting and they feel they can carry them out to an acceptable (if not perfect) level. It may mean that other things (which may be more mundane or less stimulating to the person involved, but still important – like cleaning the home) aren't done, and others things never get finished.

Who can't relate to at least one of these? See how easy it can be for clutter to build up and potentially get out of control. As Cherry Rudge explains: 'Perhaps perfectionism was one of the reasons why my dad was quite poor at expressing himself (he didn't know what to say, so he didn't say anything), even though he was constantly saying to us "You must communicate."

'My dad's perfectionism and controlling ways – combined with the fact that I now believe I probably have ADHD – turned me into a perfectionist for a very long time, with low self-esteem and lack of confidence, and a lifelong mental health condition which will probably always be with me. Fortunately – after having had CBT (which worked as a one-off as I knew what was wrong, but certainly isn't the "cure-all therapy" for all mental health conditions), a year of psychotherapy and having discovered nonviolent communication (NVC) – I now consider myself to be a recovering perfectionist. NVC, as the name suggests, is a mode of communication that uses empathy and compassion rather confrontation in order to connect with others [see <nvc-uk.com>].

'Not only does it make life much easier for me, it enables me

to give perfectionist people – and family members affected by
hoarding – a light at the end of the tunnel too.'

Control

Having and feeling a lack of control seems to be a recurring theme
in relation to hoarding. Hoarding provides control as well as a sense
of security and a feeling of safety for many people with hoarding
difficulties. It acts as a protective shield, a form of insulation, a cave.
If people feel their safety is being threatened, this can provoke a
real need to control their possessions, which is why it is important
to consult with any individual you are trying to help before even
touching anything. I worked with one woman whose very com-
plicated life was further compounded by breast cancer, as a result
of which both of her breasts had to be removed. This was just one
aspect of her life over which she had no control. She now recognizes that her hoarding implies an attempt to assert control over
her life, and she is working towards knowing what she can control,
and accepting that she cannot control everything.

Churning

Churning is the act of moving things round the house without
actually getting rid of anything. It can be a frustrating activity for
family and friends to watch as a hoarder moves bags and boxes of
items from upstairs to downstairs, raising hopes that he or she will
actually chuck them out, only to have them sit in the living room or
hall for another few years. Churning involves things being moved,
sorted, organized and tidied on a constant basis in an effort to find
things when the hoarder wants them and try and provide clear
spaces. What churning *isn't* is throwing things away.

Quite often I have heard stories where spaces have been cleared,
only for other areas to become more cluttered as possessions are
moved from one room to another without any of them being
discarded.

2

Why do people hoard?

There are various reasons why people hoard; I've already touched on some of them in Chapter 1. Hoarding expert Dr Gail Steketee of Boston University, co-author with psychologist Dr Randy Frost of several books including *Stuff: Compulsive Hoarding and the Meaning of Things* (see 'Further reading'), says that there can be a number of contributing factors, including:

- being brought up in a chaotic or confusing home, or moving frequently;
- cognitive issues that affect decision making and problem solving;
- attention deficit disorder;
- anxiety and/or depression;
- excessive guilt about waste;
- genetics and family history, given that hoarding behaviours often tend to run in families.

It's well documented that hoarding tendencies can be triggered by certain life events. Research indicates that trauma, as well as learnt behaviour from being raised in a hoarded home, can contribute to hoarding tendencies. The death of a loved one, divorce, eviction or losing one's possessions in a fire can all contribute, according to researchers at the Mayo Clinic, the medical research group based in Rochester, Minnesota. Dr Jessica Grisham of the University of New South Wales found that the link between hoarding behaviour and traumatic events, such as losing a partner or child, is especially important when people develop hoarding tendencies in later life, particularly when it follows soon after the loss. For others, hoarding can be a way of coping with an emotional upset, and can act as a form of emotional insulation.

People also hoard because of perfectionism. Perfectionists generally procrastinate through fear of making the wrong decision, which leads to indecision and respectively to keeping everything 'just in case', the result of which is clutter.

Hoarding issues can be triggered by deprivation – by 'not having a lot' when growing up, or from having had a frugal childhood in which nothing was ever thrown away. People with such childhoods consequently make up for this later on in life as a substitute for the feeling of having been denied books, toys, clothes, even friendships. Lack of meaningful relationships can trigger hoarding, which in turn leads to social isolation, the items concerned taking on a heightened importance in a person's life to fill a void and act as a replacement for interpersonal relationships.

Some people hoard for aesthetic and artistic reasons – because they appreciate and find real joy in the way objects look, or in their colour, shape, the way an ornament might reflect in certain light, the texture and feel. Objects for artists can take on a complex meaning and can be hoarded for the furthering of their art. You are probably familiar with art exhibitions in which artists have used objects to represent their artistic self – from unmade beds to crisp packets and tins of baked beans.

People also hoard for sentimental reasons, to help recapture a time when life felt good and secure. We worked in one woman's home which represented for her happier times in the 1970s, and the flat was stuck in that era. It was if time stood still for her after that decade, which was when her husband passed away.

In no particular order, the various factors that contribute to hoarding disorder can largely be categorized under the following headings.

Abuse

We have met a few people who suffered abuse during their childhood. In the main the abuse was psychological, but often people who have suffered sexual and physical abuse will be susceptible to hoarding behaviours. One man we worked with had been regularly beaten by his adoptive father. As a result, in his later years Nick collected items which represented beauty to him and quite often they were unusual, even unique. He went to meticulous lengths to display these items, and it gave him great pleasure in terms of admiring them, but they greatly impinged on his living conditions not only as a result of the scale but also the weight of his collection. He lived in a block of flats, which brought concerns about health and safety for his neighbours. He was attracted to car boot sales and would frequently come back with cash registers, coffee machines, and musical items. Nick was acquiring stuff to substitute for an abusive father who both hit him as a boy and denied him toys and love.

In our experience, people who hoard report a greater lifetime incidence of having possessions taken by force, forced sexual activity or of physical treatment during childhood. Abuse can take more subtle forms, too, and indeed may be quite unintentional, the person's parents having acted as they thought best. Secrecy or lack of openness is common. Lack of consultation about domestic changes has led to hoarding behaviours later on in life – for example, some people remember not being told they would not be returning to their old school or that they were moving house, or perhaps a favourite toy was sold or disposed of without their knowledge. The parents may not have meant to hurt their child, but the wounds are long-lasting.

Bereavement

Research suggests that bereavement is the most common contributor to hoarding behaviour. We have quite often met with people who are so consumed with grief over the loss of a loved one that they cannot bear to remove any items associated with the person who has died, and they may also shop and collect items to fill the void created by their loss. Miscarriage, the loss of a pet, the end of a relationship – all contribute to a sense of loss, grief and sadness. One woman we worked with, who had suffered a miscarriage more than 20 years ago, regularly bought baby clothes during the sales, and only just recently has she managed to stop. Coming to terms with grief can be challenging, and grief manifests itself in many forms.

Childhood issues

We have spoken to many people who have experienced unhappy episodes during their childhood, such as lack of love from their parents, being brought up in a strict and sterile home, or a sense of loneliness stemming from a lack of parental interaction or of siblings to play with. A few of our clients are themselves children, and while we cannot say that children are more likely to engage in hoarding behaviours, there is some evidence to suggest that they may be more prone to it. Some people have described feeling oppressed by their over-controlling parents, recalling their lack of freedom to act spontaneously and play freely.

Chronic disorganization

Chronic disorganization and a chaos of clutter can contribute to a hoarded home. I cannot stress enough how important it is to identify whether someone's home is hoarded because of emotional difficulties or whether the house presents as hoarded because the occupants are chronically disorganized and simply have not spent any time throwing things away. Quite often people will buy a replacement for something that they cannot find within their cluttered homes. In one home we worked in, a woman owned seven pairs of secateurs. She lacked the ability to allocate a home for her belongings and put items back there, which resulted in her difficulty in finding anything. I sometimes support my clients by acting as their 'blinkers', remaining quiet and unassuming, which helps them to stop becoming distracted and to stay focused on the task in hand.

Chronic overwhelm

Many of us feel overwhelmed at times, especially when we are experiencing a challenging and difficult situation, and it is a very common feeling among people with hoarding difficulties. For hoarders, the feeling of being overwhelmed can be all-consuming, and consequently many hoarders avoid situations where what we refer to as the 'overwhelm' will contribute to their circumstances. Feeling overwhelmed prohibits us from dealing with day-to-day challenges, and for someone with clutter, the thought of even contemplating dealing with it contributes further to that feeling. This is why many hoarders churn (move things around the house without actually getting rid of anything). We churn emotionally as well as physically as we turn things over and over in our homes and our minds.

Collecting

As children we are often encouraged to collect; from stamps, football stickers or postcards to shells from our holidays. We are encouraged to collect mementos from excursions, holidays and special occasions. Memory boxes are purchased, shelves assembled and display cabinets filled.

We are quite often asked what the difference is between a collector and a hoarder. One answer is that while both hoarders and collectors place value on their possessions, collectors will typically display their possessions in a proud and organized way and spend time and energy on their collection. A collection becomes a hoarding issue when it impacts adversely on the use of the functional areas of their home, when it becomes impossible to organize possessions easily and rooms cannot be used for their intended purpose.

Mental health issues

Mental health conditions directly relating to clutter, hoarding and disorganization are many and varied. They include personality disorders, schizophrenia, anorexia, fibromyalgia, dyslexia, dyspraxia, learning difficulties, brain injuries, dementia, cancer, arthritis and COPD, among other anxiety-based disorders, and I detail the main ones below:

Depression

Depression, including post-natal depression, is very common among people who hoard, and I know many people with clinical depression who are also are affected by hoarding. This can have a powerful impact on their motivation and engagement with their environment, as a depressed state results in low energy, difficulty in staying motivated and poor concentration. Hoarding has also been linked with bipolar disorder. The 'highs' can lead to shopping sprees, or the amassing of items for a collection of books, ornaments and so on, while the 'lows' may make it more difficult to be organized and to have the energy to throw things away. The more severe the level of bipolar disorder, the more severe the hoarding is likely to be, some research suggests.

Obsessive–compulsive disorder (OCD)

OCD affects people in different ways, but according to the NHS website it can be characterized by four main steps:

- obsession – an unwanted, intrusive and often distressing thought, image or urge repeatedly enters your mind;
- anxiety – the obsession provokes a feeling of intense anxiety or distress;
- compulsion – you feel driven to perform repetitive behaviours or acts as a result of the anxiety and distress caused by the obsession;
- temporary relief – the compulsive behaviour temporarily relieves the anxiety, but the obsession and anxiety soon returns, causing the cycle to begin again.

A few people who experience the effects of OCD find that their compulsive behaviours and fears trigger hoarding. A fear of contamination leads, for example, to the inability to tackle the post, to throw away rotten food, or to handle anything entering their homes from outside.

Lizzie

Lizzie, who had depression, OCD and schizophrenia, did not like anything being moved and if it was, it had to be put back in the same place. She was obsessive about lining up cigarette packets beneath one cushion of her sofa, as well as lining up used lighters within inches of her ashtray, next to where she sat and smoked. We tackled the hoard of cigarette packets by suggesting that as soon as she finished a packet, she should put it straight in the rubbish bin, and we explained the fire hazards to her. Lizzie recognized that her behaviour had become a ritual and understood that for her own safety she had developed a habit of putting her cigarette packets without thinking under the cushion of the sofa, and that this needed to be replaced by a new discipline of putting them in the rubbish bin.

Lizzie was also preoccupied with buying potatoes. She developed a compulsion which involved stacking up the potatoes she bought neatly in the kitchen – not only on the kitchen counter but, once that was full, on the floor. Unfortunately, she never cooked them as she was worried that her cat would burn itself with the heat of the hob of her oven. She did not use the hob for anything else. Her anxiety over her cat hurting itself far outweighed her desire to cook the potatoes she so craved. The potatoes would rot over time and she could not face picking them up;

she became very anxious about handling them even with rubber gloves. She recognized that the rotten potatoes produced a vile smell as well as an obnoxious fluid that spread across her kitchen floor. In time, Lizzie was persuaded to dispense with the stored potatoes, and to replace them with baking potatoes which she could safely cook in the oven.

Forming new habits

There'a a famous saying that if you do something enough times, it becomes a habit. A 2012 study at University College London described how habits are formed through a process called 'context-dependent repetition', in which we become almost conditioned to performing behaviours at certain times and in certain places, for example having a snack as soon as we get home every evening after work. It's possible to form a new habit, such as drinking a glass of water instead, but the researchers emphasized that repetition of the behaviour is the key, rather than carrying it out for a set amount of time (the period studied was commonly either 21 or 66 days). In other words, 'Repeat, repeat, repeat', and stay strong – don't give up.

Attention-deficit/hyperactivity disorder (ADHD)

Many people I work with have trouble staying focused on a given task and find it a challenge to maintain the attention needed to complete it. I have come across more and more people who, even if undiagnosed, are affected by both ADHD and hoarding difficulties. Not only do they have difficulty in sorting their possessions but they are also prone to impulse buying. I call the people I work with who are affected by ADHD 'butterflies' as they are prone to flit from one area of interest to another.

Often people with ADHD find it difficult throw things away – not necessarily because of an emotional attachment to their belongings but because they find the thought process of deciding what to keep and what to throw away completely overwhelming. People with ADHD quite often don't see the mess, but recognize their difficulty in finding things because of it. The idea of putting an object in a cupboard feels like sending it into a black hole. Many of the people I work with don't like to pile items up, as they feel anxious about not knowing what is at the bottom of the pile. They like things to be visible, and they spread their possessions out horizontally rather than vertically. One lady I work with uses cat litter trays to house papers that need either actioning, filing or reading. The papers are not necessarily in order, but she can see them and move the trays around the house.

How can you help someone who both hoards and has ADHD? Remove distractions, perhaps put on some calming music, introduce some time management skills, use a timer and provide reminders. Post-it notes and clear labelling are useful tools. Chapter 5 provides some useful tips.

Figure 1 overleaf is designed to show the chaotic nature of what's going on in the ADHD mind, and how debilitating ADHD can be.

Autistic spectrum disorder (ASD)

Research suggests that people on the autistic spectrum commonly have special interests and hobbies which in turn can lead them to put together specific collections. For some people, this activity may be obsessive, while in others it may not. Sometimes it is difficult to determine whether hoarding is related to OCD or to behaviours associated with ASD. You may ask how you deal with someone with ASD who exhibits hoarding behaviours. From my experience and knowledge, it is about setting limits and boundaries, and pointing out the implications of the person's hoarding and the impact it may have on his or her health and safety. Clear communication is key, along with step-by-step actions and bite-sized interventions.

John

Social services contacted me asking for my help with a family who were being threatened by eviction because of the clutter in their new flat – especially around John's bedroom. Mum was depressed, going through a divorce, and John, a young teenager, had ASD and was also anxious and depressed as a result of the change to his family life and the need to adjust to his new bedroom.

The bedroom was a sea of rubbish – empty fizzy drink cans and crisp packets, sweet wrappers, batteries, dirty clothes, towels, pizza boxes and books. John did not want his mother invading his personal space, but he let me in and we talked about how we would need to clear his items off the carpet so that the landlord would be happy about retaining their tenancy. The key to helping was to be specific in what tasks were

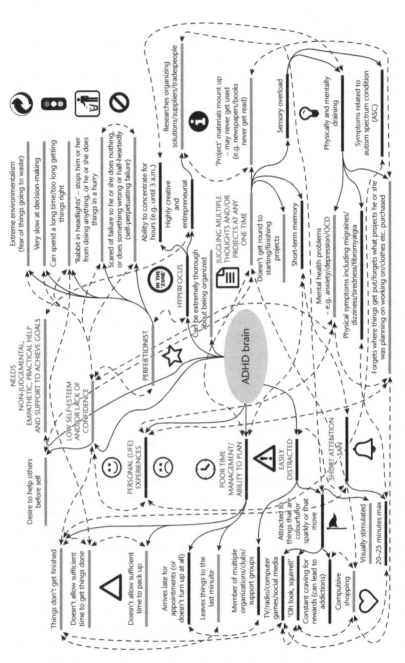

Figure 1 The planning and organizing chaos of the ADHD brain

needed to tackle the mess. Both John and his mother were too over-whelmed to tidy it.

I worked with John over four sessions. Rather than just bringing in bin bags and throwing everything away, at first we looked at the pizza boxes, then the crisp packets and other food wrappers. I explained to John that the reasons for addressing the food items were to eliminate the possibility of any problems with mice. I then asked his mother to buy John a rubbish bin for his room and we agreed that meals were to be eaten at the dining room table, and that he should not allow pizza boxes in his bedroom. At our next session, we dealt with batteries and fizzy drink cans (both of which were to be recycled). At this session we also suggested that Mum ask John for any cans to be recycled from his room each week. At a further session we worked on dirty clothes and asked his mother if she could provide John with his own laundry bag. Towels too were picked up and assigned a hook on the back of John's bedroom door. At the last session we addressed clean clothes and allo-cated them drawers clearly labelled for his socks, T-shirts and underwear.

At each session I checked with John that he was happy with me doing all this in his space, and that he was happy about the decisions we were making about his belongings. On some occasions he asked that we stop and on others he was happy to carry on. When we eventually brought the vacuum cleaner in to clean the floor, he was very happy and proud to show his mum his room.

Clear boundaries about what food items were allowed in his room were established, and structures and routines put in place with respect to rubbish, recycling and laundry. The tenancy is no longer at threat and John feels more secure and empowered about managing his personal space.

Much of our role in helping the people we work with is to come up with practical solutions, many of which are creative and tailored and unique to each individual's circumstances. I feel John's story is particularly important as it is not a story of hoarding per se, but of problems that present themselves as a hoarding issue, one which with the right interventions and strategies was successfully managed. Although this approach might not work for everyone – as I've repeatedly stressed, this is an individual issue – I feel that this story is a useful one to share.

Trauma and crime

Both PTSD (Post-Traumatic Stress Disorder) and any other trauma experienced in life can contribute to a hoarded and chaotic home. Events including accident and disaster, miscarriage, burglary, sexual attack, sudden death within a family, even divorce, can all precipitate hoarding behaviours as a safety mechanism. It is as if the people concerned are trying to create a barrier or buffer against further disaster.

Some people who have been affected by a crime can begin to exhibit hoarding behaviours as part of their coping response. We know of one gentleman who had been attacked quite brutally in the street and his rucksack, which contained his laptop, diary and wallet, stolen from him. The victim could not provide sufficient evidence and a description of the attacker to the police for the crime to be solved. In response to the incident, the victim developed an obsessive routine of reading and collecting local newspapers in the hope that he might pick up on some information that he could give to the police in relation to his attacker. His flat now presents as a hoarded home filled with potential paper evidence.

Empty nest syndrome

So often as parents we become solely focused on our roles of raising our children, from the early days of potty training to teaching our older teenagers how to iron shirts ready for their first office job. As parents it is easy to become absorbed in that role and forget what life was like before children. But, in the same way we should plan for retirement, we need to plan for life after children. The effect on a home once the children have flown the nest can be dramatic, leaving a vacuum in which we find ourselves with more time, less dependency and more questioning 'Who am I?' Some parents may feel the need to rediscover themselves as individuals with their own hobbies, interests and talents; others may lack the confidence to return to work. They may try to fill the void by acquiring stuff, so that often unhealthy shopping habits develop, resulting in hoarding behaviours.

Another related issue can be the temptation to hold on to the possessions that grown-up children have left at home, and which have simply never been sorted through. Boxes of school work, musical instruments, clothes and books can all pile up, consuming a surprising amount of space. This is an issue that obviously needs to be addressed with your child.

Filling the gap

When our emotional needs are not being met, we can be prone, perhaps, to over-eating or to over-spending to fill a void in our lives. Hoarding can act as compensation for a lack of close relationships, an unhappy marriage, loneliness, low self-worth or dents in self-esteem. A divorce, for example, may well precipitate a need to hoard and acquire in response to the breakdown of the relationship. If we feel we are not being sufficiently emotionally nourished, we may seek comfort in hoarding and acquiring, just as we seek solace in over-eating. Retail therapy, buying extraneous items because they are reduced, visiting car boot sales and charity shops, are all common, and with more online opportunities to buy, such as Freecycle and eBay, the temptation to acquire more things is strong.

In addition to partnerships, wider emotional issues may include generally not feeling protected, safe or cared for, or not feeling sufficiently loved, accepted or stable. This does not apply only to personal relationships but is equally valid in our professional life. As people, we need to feel fulfilled, supported, included and accepted, not only in our personal lives but also at work.

Hunger

My father lived through the Second World War and was evacuated from Poland as a child. He remembers feeling hungry at the time, and this left an impression on him as an adult, a husband and a father. He hated wasting food, and we as children had to eat everything on our plates. If we missed even a grain of rice or two, this was spotted and we had to eat it. From our childhood garden, each blackberry from the bush had to be picked and frozen, apples gathered and chestnuts collected and distributed among family and friends. Any waste that my mother incurred was hidden from my father.

Hoarding of food in response to hunger is well known among the survivors of Nazi concentration camps. They went on later to hoard not only food, but clothes and money as well. I have witnessed an abundance of bread rolls and fruit laid out on the dining tables of Jewish residential care homes for survivors of the Nazi camps. The staff felt that having this abundance of food on the table would reduce the anxiety experienced by the residents, which had resulted from not having enough to eat in the past, and that they would feel less compelled to take food to their rooms if they knew that there was 'enough' in the kitchen and dining room.

Redundancy

In the current economic climate, and following the recent recession, redundancy is common. We have worked with individuals who have experienced the impact of being made redundant not just from one job but from two or three within their professional careers. The psychological effects of redundancy can bring about a tremendous sense of loss – not only a financial loss, but also a loss of status resulting from the absence of full-time employment. Quite often our careers define our sense of purpose, and the shock of redundancy can be life-changing. Feelings of overwhelm can lead to unusual spending habits, and hoarding can help soothe the anxiety and alleviate a need to stockpile due to financial concerns.

Eric and Joan

Quite often married couples have opposing characteristics. One may be tidy, the other messy; one good with money, the other a spendthrift. In some marriages, however, the partners are two of a kind. You may wonder what this has to do with hoarding, but when a compulsive buyer and an 'I might need it one day', chronically disorganized hoarder live together in one house and both share a love of dogs, the outcome can be similar to that of Eric and Joan. The couple, who were childless, had more than a dozen Miniature Schnauzer dogs living with them. Their home ended up congested with clutter, so that the couple were barely able to see from one end of the living room to the other. A nurse who was a family friend contacted me quite soon after Joan died of cancer. As Joan's life was ending, she apologized to Eric for all the mess and the dogs that he had to take care of.

After Joan died, Eric poured his energies into rehousing the dogs and then was left with a house full of stuff – unopened packages of clothes, pens, brooches, cups, aprons – mainly featuring pictures of Miniature Schnauzers. Eric too had his own hoard – every broken tap or broken lampshade would be stored in the attic. Both Eric and Joan had been only children, and on the death of both sets of parents, their belongings had been stored in the attic and the summer house. Eric had built the summer house himself. It was beautiful, made of cedar wood and located at the bottom of the garden, an ideal place to sit and muse. He delighted in telling us that at one time it had revolved. We had never heard of a revolving summer house, but then understood that it revolved for the purposes of capturing the sun and shade. Sadly, though, Eric told us that it had stopped revolving many years ago thanks to the weight of the couple's belongings.

Eric's garage was full of broken lawnmowers, rusty tools, and the remnants of his and Joan's lives with the dogs. We started by donating more than half a dozen dog crates to the Dogs Trust, along with various bags bursting with dogs' clothes, leads, bowls and balls and an assortment of toys and flea and worm treatments. We recognised that Eric would not be able to cope with a quick and dramatic clearout, or the 'bring in a skip' approach. He would, however, benefit from a slow but sure approach to reclaiming his space, dealing with his wife's estate and the contents of his home. Eric needed gradually to come to terms with his grief, part of which involved being able to better understand his wife's compulsion to shop.

We worked with Eric slowly and regularly over the course of two years. Eric and Joan had been too embarrassed to ask a plumber in to deal with the taps in the bathroom, which had been dripping incessantly and furiously for several years. Their water bills had been extortionate. Eric had managed to reduce the bill by turning the water off and each morning he would take his tool to the mains in the road to turn it on again. He liked the idea of having the taps fixed and once we had managed to sort and clear enough space we contacted Lisa, a local plumber who we knew would not judge or comment on the condition of his house. She not only replaced the taps but the bathroom sink too (the taps had become welded to it). On our next visit, when we asked how Eric he was enjoying having water on tap, he remarked that he was at a loss to know how to deal with no longer having his morning and evening routine of turning the water on and off at the mains.

We worked on making both the small changes that Eric wanted and also those needed to address the damp, mould and mildew in the bedrooms that had been used as storage units.

After some time Eric developed Alzheimer's, and he explained that he was happy to go into a care home and sell his house and let go of his stuff. We helped him sell and clear his belongings, and downsize his wardrobe and books. On our many visits to the care home to ensure that Eric was involved and kept in the loop as to the destination of his belongings, it became apparent that he was happy to leave his stuff and his past behind. Eric was now much more motivated and eagerly told me of his intention to learn to play his clarinet. The house is now empty, having been sold, and Eric is quite happy with his clarinet and a few precious books and photos. He says he feels not only liberated but also relieved that he can now be taken care of without the challenges of living in a house full of stuff. And he plays his clarinet regularly!

3

Seeing the problem: learning to visualize clutter

Clutter Image Ratings (CIRs) are a way to identify the scale of hoarding. One major advantage of the ratings is that they are impersonal, removing personal perception and judgement of clutter. This chapter looks at how to use the Clutter Image Ratings, who uses them, and the importance of these visual elements in accurately assessing clutter.

Clutter blindness

I have met many people who are initially unaware of the extent of their clutter, in the same way that we remain unaware of gaining weight until we can no longer fit into our favourite pair of jeans. We may then blame the washing machine or dryer for having shrunk them, until perhaps we try another pair on and realize that because we have been overeating we no longer fit into our favourite clothes! We might then find we have to adjust the hole on our watch strap, rings may become too tight on our fingers and our winter coat might not button up properly.

With clutter and hoarding, similar scenarios will occur, and we can lose the ability to retrieve, find or place items any longer – simply because we have run out of room. I know people who have erected tents in their gardens, not to sleep in but to store additional items. Shower cubicles and cars are adopted as additional space to house their treasured stuff.

In the hoarding world we frequently use the term *clutter blindness*. Visual images can be very powerful in terms of putting this phenomenon in context and gaining some objective reality on the situation. Just as we use photos to spur us into losing weight, so photos of rooms can be very effective. We can use them as a way of confronting reality, as well as using them as motivational tools. It is not that hoarders are blind to their clutter, it is that they become accustomed to it, and ultimately the pile of papers that was once a few inches high is now well over a foot high and has become part of the norm. I compare clutter to ivy. Ivy has a way of creeping through the windows without being noticed, in through your neighbour's door, twisting its way round cables and choking other plants. Suddenly the ivy has taken over. Clutter acts in the same way.

We all have our own opinions as to what is tidy and what is not, just as we have our own thoughts and beliefs on what is minimalist, sleek and stark and what we consider cosy, comfy and lived-in. We also have different standards in terms of what we consider clean and what we consider to be dirty and messy.

Before and after photos can be inspiring for hoarders who have been through the clearing process and may help them maintain the 'after', reminding them that they do not want to go back to the 'before'.

The Clutter Image Ratings

Clutter Image Ratings were developed by US professionals Gail Steketee and Randy Frost in 2007 as a rating scale for the assessment and measuring of hoarding and clutter. They are a pictorial tool which measures the level of clutter within a person's home. The pictures are numbered from 1 = 'no clutter' to 9 = 'severe clutter' for the three main rooms (kitchen, living room, bedroom) in a typical home.

The scale is easy to see, measure and administer. The fire services use the ratings and refer to them as 'fire loadings'. CIRs are very effective when we are working with professionals and we need to communicate the scale and severity of the hoard without being subjective. By using this scale, much of the subjectivity is taken out of rating the level of clutter.

Being able objectively to rate the level of clutter also makes the ratings useful as an outcome measure, and to demonstrate the progress made with the person you are helping. We encourage everyone to use CIRs in order to avoid confusion in the perception of what a home looks like to friends, family, hoarders and related organizations. For details of the clutter image ratings, please visit: <hoardingdisordersuk.org/wp-content/uploads/2014/01/clutter-image-ratings.pdf>.

4

Decluttering techniques and tips

This chapter offers some decluttering tips that have proven to be very effective for people with hoarding behaviours. If you are the hoarder, and you feel ready to start unloading some of your hoard, then read on, but remember, take things at your own pace, and do stop and celebrate each small achievement. If you're trying to help a hoarder, you will also benefit from reading this chapter, and there is more advice in Chapter 5, 'How to help someone who hoards'.

There are numerous books and online tips, courses and media articles on decluttering. Decluttering and living with less seems to be very much in vogue. In December 2015, Marie Kondo, the author of the bestselling book *The Life-Changing Magic of Tidying*, which has sold over five million copies, was recognized by *Time* magazine as one of the 100 most influential people in the world. The Konmari (Marie Kondo's nickname) method is to declutter and sort stuff by categories, and encourages festivals of blitzing sessions of people's possessions. We have read the book and discussed the Konmari method at our hoarding support groups, but whereas the book provides some excellent tips, for hoarders her approach is far too radical and overwhelming.

There is a difference between what we might call a clutterbug and a hoarder. Hoarders tend to have strong emotional attachments to most of their possessions and have great difficulty in throwing anything away; they are often embarrassed to have visitors and are quite often unable to use rooms for their intended use. Clutterbugs do not necessarily have the same emotional issues; they can be easily persuaded and motivated to address their clutter, which can be the result of simply never throwing anything away, or can stem from the laziness and/or chronic disorganization that results in what looks like a hoarded home.

Where do we start?

When we work with people who have a hoarding problem, we always start by talking about their individual frustrations and challenges in their living environment. This then helps determine where we start. So, if you are trying to deal with your own hoarding, decide on something that would make a real difference to your life. Usually this will be a small space, the least emotional area of the house, one that will provide maximum impact and produce a positive visual effect. We often start in kitchens; for one lady, simply concentrating on one area of a kitchen table meant that she could use the table to eat her meals from, rather than the tray she had been using. She has made a commitment to protect this space and values the decluttered area – though her husband quite often sees the space as an opportunity to fill it up again as a way of redistributing the clutter! There is as much work to be done in maintaining a clear space as there is in decluttering a space.

Keep it simple

Simple questions and clear quotes can help the decision-making process and the choices to be made with regard to possessions. Here are some simple yet affirmative prompts and quotations:

- Remember the 3 Cs – chuck, cherish, charity.
- Use the principle 'One in, one out'.
- Everything in its place, and a place for everything.
- Would I replace it if it went?
- Would I miss it?
- When was the last time I used it?
- Does it enhance my life in any way?
- How many do I have?
- Is it broken?
- Is it out of date?
- What is the worst thing that could happen if I let it go?
- Anything that evokes negative thoughts can be disposed of. Why be reminded of bad times?
- 'If in doubt – chuck it out.'

The OHIO rule

OHIO is an abbreviation for 'Only Handle It Once'. This rule is very effective in the workplace as a time management tool; for example, when dealing with emails. The same rule can also be applied to decluttering homes and saves time on decision making and possible avoidance tactics: 'I'll think about it later', and so on. The concept is to pick up an item, and decide at once:

- Does it stay? If so, decide where should it live.
- Should it be recycled? Then put it in the recycling bin.
- Should it go to charity? Put it in the charity bag.
- Should it be thrown away? Put it in the rubbish bin, or put it outside to go to the recycling unit.

The above list is one that you can select from and add to. If the options above feel too drastic or cut and dried, then maybe consider the next option.

The 'keep for a week' rule

A gentleman we regularly worked with devised this rule. His life was busy and fulfilled and he found joy and excitement in new technology; although committed to the decluttering process, he quite often needed time to think about whether he could let go of any item. Having a box or pile of 'doubtful' items takes the pressure off for some people. If there is an element of doubt over whether or not to let go of an item or to keep it, it is best not to pressurize yourself but to create a 'dilemma pile', and try to 'keep for a week'. This should allow you to process the item and to decide whether or not you want to keep it.

However, do be mindful of the fact while you are sorting that the dilemma pile should not be the biggest one. If it is beginning to look like it is, then it might be worth delving into why you are hesitating so much about reaching a decision. We put brightly coloured Post-it notes on the items that are to 'keep for a week'. Sometimes within a cluttered home it is difficult to see things, so the use of bright colour highlights the areas that are in question.

Grouping and categories

It is important to simplify clutter-clearing sessions. Sorting through just one area of a room ensures that you are not overwhelmed with having to process many categories of items, and means that the decision-making process is much easier. Another way to conduct a session is by grouping items together. This really helps; it makes the decision-making process much easier when items are brought together in one place. It is far easier to process your clutter if you are only reviewing one category of it rather than having to deal with a mish-mash of different items.

You might want to decide that you are tackling clothes first, or paperwork, or your collection of dolls that is scattered all over the house. If this feels too overwhelming, break the process down even further – for example, instead of tackling all your paperwork, focus on one aspect of it. Once you have established that you are reviewing, say, magazines, bringing all the magazines together from around the home helps in assessing the volume realistically, and decisions can be made more quickly.

Clutter is essentially delayed decision making, so to empower and help yourself with this makes the process that much less challenging. Remain focused on one area, recognize when you are flagging and take a break. Some people set a timer for 15 or 20 minutes and review their progress at the end of that time.

Liz

Liz had a vast collection of hats, including straw summer hats, caps, fur hats, fascinators, hats for weddings, and top hats. They reminded her of her theatrical days in the past, and she also enjoyed wearing them. They were scattered around the house. We brought them all together, and by doing so enabled her to assess her collection and decide which straw summer hat she would like to keep, which one was past its best, which was bobbly and which ones were no longer in fashion.

Establishing rules

We have found that the establishment of certain rules will usually make sessions less challenging. Rules help break down the decision-making process even further and provide clear criteria for decisions, which in turn helps prevent you being overwhelmed. For example, many hoarders have huge amounts of clothes, and can't begin to decide which ones to keep. So, when reviewing clothes, a simple rule would be that those which no longer fit go out. For one gentleman, if his trousers had a 42-inch waist and below, they were deemed too small and could therefore go to charity. Another rule could be to do with how long objects have been in the house. In the same gentleman's case, we applied the rule to magazines over two years old and so recycled any over this age.

Other rules that may be helpful to you include the following:

- Out of date food is to go.
- Newspapers that are more than *x* years old are to be recycled.
- Magazines that are more than *x* years old are to be recycled.
- Food containers with no lids are to be recycled.
- Out of date medicines to go back to the pharmacy to be safely destroyed.
- Chipped or broken crockery (because it can be dangerous and cause infection) is to be recycled.
- Junk mail is to go in the recycling bin.
- Old catalogues are to be recycled – keep the most up-to-date Argos catalogue and dispose of the older versions.
- Put out any clothes that don't fit.

You might also want to apply a rule to get rid of the following:

- broken appliances
- unused toiletries
- unwanted presents
- old receipts – date to be identified
- old bills
- old to-do lists
- old shopping lists
- old Christmas cards
- shoes with holes in.

Create a picture

We feel that setting objectives can seem an imposition to the people we are helping. We prefer to engage with them by 'creating a vision', as it feels more tangible and less pressured. Motivation to clear clutter can be lacking if there are no clear pictures and visions to aim for, so to establish and review visions and aims is important to the person's ongoing commitment to reclaiming his or her home.

So, what vision do you have for your house? What single change would make the most difference to you? Try and visualize it in your mind's eye, or even draw a sketch (it doesn't have to be a work of art), whether it's a clear hallway, a tidy bathroom, or a bed you can access without having to move everything off it first.

Jane and Paul – vision of a kitchen table

We have been working with a married couple, Jane and Paul, whose kitchen table has been cluttered for many years with an assortment of items, many of which are nothing to do with the kitchen. It became very evident very soon that Paul was more resistant to clearing the kitchen table than his wife, who needed to use the table more than he did.

After a few frustrating sessions when they proved resistant to taking action, the couple agreed to meet for a coffee away from their home. This provided both the couple and us with the opportunity to contemplate and discuss their home more objectively, and it became apparent that to clear the kitchen table completely would leave the husband extremely anxious. The kitchen table acted as his 'control centre', and with declining eyesight and mobility, he depended on it as the area where he was most able to access important items. This meant, however, that his wife could not use the table either for preparing or eating meals. We suggested that perhaps we could clear just one area of the table that would allow his wife to do this. They agreed that this was achievable and we spent the next session clearing a space. Weeks on, the area remains clear and the space has become one that is fiercely protected, hugely respected, and a reminder of the benefits of a clear space.

Health and safety

At each session, it is important to address any potential health and safety issues, including trip hazards and potential avalanches as items that have been piled up start tumbling down. In particular, it is important to be mindful of fire hazards. Many hoarded homes have 'daisy chains' of extension leads, precariously balanced electrical items, locked windows and blocked exits; paperwork is kept near the cooker and there is an excess of flammable materials. Additionally, it is important to address any areas that cannot be accessed with ease – for example, a bed to sleep in, somewhere to wash up, the use of a kettle, being able to answer the door.

The fire services are active in addressing hoarding, and free 'Safe and Well' visits are available. During a visit, free smoke alarms can be installed and practical hazard reduction tips and advice provided. The fire services can be a very important ally. For further information and guidance, please visit The Chief Fire Officers Association (see 'Useful addresses').

Some dos and don'ts

If you are attempting to deal with your own clutter, do:

- take things at your own pace;
- think about what is acceptable to you;
- be clear about what you are doing;
- provide yourself with appropriate tools such as bags or boxes. For example, one for put where it belongs, one for charity, one for Freecycle and one for rubbish;
- think about safety. For example, if there was a fire or other emergency, what would be your route out?
- think about who will provide the support you need;
- let any helpers know what they can and cannot do or touch, and where they can go;
- stop when you get overwhelmed, tidy up after yourself as much as possible, and walk away;
- celebrate the space you have cleared. Buy some flowers for it, or enjoy using it again;
- reward yourself for what you've achieved (but not by buying any more!), for example with a hot chocolate in a nice café, or a walk.

Don't:

- try and do too much at once – start with sessions of 15 minutes or half an hour, and build up;
- start without being prepared with the tools required;
- just move things around ('churning' – see page 15). If you are not ready to let things go, then focus on getting to the stage where you are.

5

How to help someone who hoards

It can be very tempting to try and help a hoarder, and if it were a matter merely of good will and energy, there would be few hoarded homes left. There are plenty of willing hands ready to help clear a cluttered home and restore the damage that may have been done by years of accumulated possessions weighing down floors, stacked against walls, and creating areas of damp and mould. The British love of house projects and DIY is well known! However, there's no doubt that helping a hoarder needs tact and the right skills – and above all, a flexible approach, one that is guided by the person you are trying to help.

So, who can help? 'Anyone' is the answer, providing you have the correct tools and skills. Someone who is trusted, discreet, non-judgemental and not overbearing. Above all, someone who is sensitive to the dignity and privacy of the person who hoards. Your fingers may be itching to clear and tidy a hoarded home, but, as this chapter will show, this is by no means always the best way.

Having a clearout

Historically, it was thought that an intense and concentrated clear-out could solve the issues of a hoarded home. With the best of intentions, family members and friends often thought they were helping by suggesting an intense declutter and tidying-up session. Landlords too have made helpful suggestions, such as offering to park a skip in front of the person's home to help clear the clutter. Some families have called in the council or local environmental health services to clear the rubbish away. All this can in fact make matters worse.

It is now more widely recognized that a forced clearout is unsustainable, too radical, and can reinforce the problem. Such a strategy can change the home environment temporarily but will not change hoarding behaviour. In fact, it is far too traumatic for the person with hoarding difficulties. Hoarders may feel lost without their clutter, and may quickly refill the space, and it's more than likely that the home will return to an even more cluttered level than before. People have compared the experience of a clearout to a sense of violation, or involuntary surgery. Some have found the experience so traumatic and unsettling that they have been unable to move forward or recover from it.

We have worked with several people who have experienced a forced clearout and who were not involved or consulted in the clearing, sorting, disposing of and decluttering of their own homes. Along with Amanda Peet, co-founder with me of Hoarding Disorders UK, I recognized that it is not just about decluttering a house and hoping the clutter will stay at bay, it's about looking at the person first and dealing with the stuff second. For any progress to be made, I cannot emphasize enough how important it is for those who exhibit hoarding behaviours to feel that they are being heard, respected and not judged.

In the following example it was family who helped. Others may prefer to get help from a trusted friend, yet others from a professional, someone outside their family or social group whom they may never see again.

Lynn's story

I used to have a hoarded house, in which none of the rooms apart from the bathroom were suitable for their original use. It was obvious that something had to be done, and that really it was down to me. I started on my own, setting a timer for 15 minutes and dealing with 'easy' items. I used to collect newspapers and magazines on the premise that there was useful information in the articles they contained, or interesting items that I had yet to read. I realized that whenever I wanted up-to-date information I would go to the internet. I enjoy reading and read books, so there was no time to read the articles I was saving. Putting newspapers and magazines into the recycling was making use of them, and was also a 'quick win' for my clearing.

My sister then started to help. She was guided by me regarding where we would clear and for how long. Most of the time she was there for support rather than dealing with items; she held containers, offered encouragement, validated my decisions and pointed out the progress I'd made. Once a fair bit of progress had been made, I felt more ready for other members of the family to come in and provide some help, though always with the support and backing of my sister.

There were hiccups along the way, and my father still has no understanding of the issues I am facing. He cannot understand why I cannot 'just throw things away', why it is so difficult to make decisions, and why it takes so long to do things. I am still struggling to deal with his inability to understand.

My dad was a major stumbling block in clearing the utility room and my bedroom. As the result of an offer of help he threw away clothes that had been put aside for washing – helpers have to be absolutely clear as to what they can and cannot touch. They also have to be clear that while maybe they cannot appreciate the value in some of the collected items, they need to respect the fact that the person who acquired them values them.

After my sister's support, the next key reassurance was that a lot of the items would go to charity shops or be recycled for future use. It has always been important to me that my things are not just thrown away – I have worked for them, chosen them and used a lot of them. If this is important to you, there are lots of places where you can repurpose your items.

One room in my house was totally devoted to teddy bears (I am an arctophile, someone who is very fond of, and usually a collector of, teddy bears). These are not stuffed toys, but properly jointed bears. Some are unique, some are valuable, some are well loved from childhood. I am in a dilemma about what to do with them. To me they are precious, and as I said previously some are actually valuable. Will my family be aware of their value once I am no longer here? I worry about this; I don't want them all thrown into a skip. Do I realize their value now, sell them and enjoy the financial gain in some other way? But I enjoy owning them, looking at the few I have not stored in boxes (this was how I cleared the room). I am slowly coming to think that others would enjoy them and considering ways in which I can achieve this.

If you have something that you regard as valuable, or has real monetary or other value, think about what is acceptable to you if you really don't have the space to keep it.

My final sticking point is clothes. I still have one room I cannot use and my bedroom is starting to grow a clothes mountain at one end. I have not yet come to think about how I will deal with the majority of these. I have made a small start and reviewed some of the clothes. I am trying to be realistic – do they fit, are they age appropriate, would I have a situation when I would wear them again? If not, they have gone to the local charity shop. I have been realistic – are they fit for sale, would someone else buy them? If not, then charity shops do collect clothing, linens, fabrics, etc. for 'rags'. They will get paid for any unwanted fabrics by weight, so these can still be useful to a charity.

Having made a good start with support from my family, I've joined a hoarding support group that has started in the area and this has proved very motivational, reassuring and supportive. The group provides a safe and secure place for people with hoarding behaviours, and those supporting them. Talks and techniques bring a new perspective to dealing with the items themselves and the feelings and behaviours involved. There are talks from Cruse on bereavement, and talks on mindfulness, fire, health and safety, and stress control. But the most useful parts of the meetings are those when people just talk to each other. Feedback from those who attend indicates that they no longer feel as if it is 'just them', that others are in a similar situation. They feel more able to discuss the issues involved, as the people attending really understand what is going on. Ideas and techniques are exchanged and these spark enthusiasm and determination. New ways of recycling and repurposing are suggested.

People are no longer isolated, and feelings of overwhelm recede so that they feel able to deal with their situation. Small steps are encouraged and achievements celebrated. Getting validation of their achievements from other members of the group seems more meaningful as these people understand the issues.

Where am I now? I have a living and dining room that are easy to clean and use; a clear, welcoming hallway; a kitchen with clear worktops, where I can start doing more of the baking and cooking that I enjoy; an upstairs bathroom and downstairs toilet that are also easy to clean and use (these were never a real problem for me, but they can be for some); a bright and mostly airy bedroom, and a bright, airy spare bedroom in which friends have been able to stay (something that has not happened since I first moved into the house 18 years ago). My spare bedroom is still full of clothes and my shed is full of boxes. I think the shed will be next on my list for clearing.

Each individual is unique

Each person's hoard is unique, and not only are people's circumstances different but their personality, make-up, beliefs, life choices and principles are all individual. You cannot apply the same set of rules and action plans to one case as you would to another. It is important to factor this in when assessing timeframes, progress and engagement. Hoarding raises a range of practical and emotional problems which need to be addressed, alongside the complexity of hoarding, as mental health disorders. Enforced decluttering will not help. It is important to know when the person you are hoping to help is ready to address his or her hoarding behaviours, and to support the person even when he or she does not feel like engaging.

Be sensitive in terms of language. You may regard a hoard as a load of old rubbish, but advice such as 'Set a match to it all' is likely at best to fall on deaf ears. If you are helping friends or family, you know what might work for them, so use the most sensitive approach. If 'chucking' is a word you know might upset them, don't use it. Not that you should rule it out – it may be one you can come back to further down the line, when trust has been built up and more 'fun' has been added to the process. Fun and an upbeat disposition are very important!

Tom

We have worked with many people with autism, and in these cases the key to a successful session is to be clear in communicating the desired outcome of the session and to work in a structured fashion. Tom hoards newspapers, wanting not only to complete the crossword puzzle but also the Sudoku puzzles. His house is overrun with publications. After meeting his support worker in her office, we agreed a plan to deal with decluttering the newspapers, junk mail and post surrounding his front door, which he has been unable to open for about six months. The outcome of our sessions was to group the newspapers together, group the junk email together and bag any personal correspondence separately. On this basis Tom could then cut out the puzzles and recycle the remainder of the newspapers.

We agreed that homework would include processing the junk mail and opening the post. So far this is working for Tom. As he also suffers from depression our sessions are kept to an hour and a half every fortnight. This isn't a typical session, but it illustrates how we have considered Tom's personal situation and the challenges he is presented with.

How best to help

The process of helping can be slow, tedious and time-consuming, and it is crucial to anyone wanting to help – whether you are a professional, a friend, a relative or a support worker – that you are aware of this. The two key qualities needed are patience and humour.

It is important to curb any excess enthusiasm and the urge to clear the clutter and organize the person's space without consulting her. You may feel that you are helping, but it is important that the person you are helping learns to make her own decisions, changes her mindset, addresses long-term habits and finds ways of organizing things that fit and suit her. What works for you doesn't necessarily work for the person you are helping. Successful decluttering includes recognizing the habits and behaviours associated with acquiring possessions, and understanding why and how clutter can accumulate. When you work with people to clear their hoarding, it's important to highlight this and to develop people's own powers of reasoning with regard to these often complex issues.

We work with an Eight-Step Plan, details of which can be accessed from the Hoarding Disorders UK website (see 'Useful addresses'). This breaks the task down into individual components such as clearing the emotional attachment to items, and finding a personal identity apart from all the belongings, as well as clearing sessions, and I've adapted some of the plan in this chapter for individual use by readers of this book. The key is empowerment. Empowerment is essential to helping hoarders to reorganize their homes. Empowerment helps people develop decision-making abilities and organizational skills, enables them to recognize hoarding behaviours, and helps them implement goal-directed strategies and planning skills. Ideally, the person should end up feeling confident about decision making.

Many people who hoard have such low self-esteem that they find it very difficult to see that they are worthy of any intervention or positive attention. Sometimes, it is very difficult to tackle the physical 'stuff' before addressing how the person's mental health can be improved. Do get the person you are seeking to help to consult his or her GP if this is the case, and take a look at Chapter 8, 'Helpful therapies'.

And do remember – a hoarded house hasn't just happened overnight. Sometimes it has taken years to reach the present level of hoarding. It's bound to take a while to return it to a clearer state.

Clutter clearing sessions – where to start

Sometimes, the first stage in clearing a very cluttered home is to create a space that acts as a processing area. For example, you could clear a table that can be used in future sessions for sorting things. Decluttering in the spring and summer months is much easier, as you can use any available outside space as a processing area, and it is less claustrophobic for both the individual and anyone helping.

Here are a few decluttering tips that have proven to be very effective when working with people who exhibit hoarding behaviours:

Start small. A corner of a table, a shelf in the hall, a treasured dresser, a bedside table – choose something contained and manageable. Starting with just one corner and committing to addressing that area will create confidence in the person you are helping, and assurance that space can be regained. It is important to reassure the person that decluttering in baby steps on a frequent and consistent basis can lead to a sustainable and improved living environment.

Set clear, manageable goals for each session. Establish what needs to be achieved at the start of a decluttering session, taking into consideration the person's personality, age, any learning difficulties and/or mental health disorders. All these factors are critical to ensuring the person you are helping will benefit from each session and that the aims are realistic to his or her demeanour and situation.

Make it regular. Schedule and commit to regular sessions, so that the process of decluttering forms part of the person's daily routine.

Adapt. Recognize and adapt different styles of working with individuals who may be affected by obsessive–compulsive disorder, those with autism/Asperger's, ADHD or schizophrenia.

Watch your language. Mirror the language the individual hoarder uses regarding his or her 'stuff' – hoarders are very sensitive to how people perceive their homes.

Never leave a room empty handed. For example, if you are on your way to the kitchen, take anything that needs to be returned there – whether for washing up or disposal.

Establish one 'landing strip'. Identify somewhere you can empty your pockets, including a place to put your keys and phone.

Useful or beautiful? William Morris, artist and textile designer, famously said, 'Have nothing in your house that you do not know to be useful or believe to be beautiful.' This can be quite influential with some people, although others may well believe that everything in their home is both useful and beautiful!

'No parking' and 'red route' areas

You may wonder what 'no parking' and 'red route' areas have to do with hoarding. It is a simple rule I establish when working with hoarders – take a look at the 'Establishing rules' section in the previous chapter (page 38), which helps break the clearing process down into more manageable chunks. No parking and red route areas are places where we agree that clutter cannot land or be parked – essentially for health and safety, so that once a congested area has been cleared, we mark it as a no parking area. It's also useful to simplify the way that you work when addressing a hoarded house, as hoarders tend to over-complicate and overthink a situation.

Perfectionism and decision-making

As we saw in Chapter 2, many hoarders are perfectionists and poor decision makers, and it is useful to recognize whether this is a trait of the person you are working with. Perfectionism can deter progress by causing us to focus too readily on insignificant details and therefore fail to see the bigger picture. It can be self-defeating, and lead not only to apathy but also inertia. Not being a perfectionist is far more productive than being one. Perfectionism can lead to procrastination and paralysis. If you wait to do something perfectly, you may never get it done at all, and helping a person undertaking the decluttering process to accept this can be a very effective way of supporting him. One example of perfectionism and procrastination in a hoarding situation would be where a person does not want to put his clothes away because they all need ironing. The reality is that it would take several hours to iron them, so rather than be distracted by the task of ironing, the non-perfectionist would put them away and then iron them as and when they are needed.

Perfectionists tend to be very critical of themselves, as well as having many limiting core beliefs – for example, the man who is an artist but is never happy with his artwork, and who as a result never finishes a piece to his own satisfaction. It needs to be asked whether he is unhappy with his work, or if his core belief that 'I can't do anything right' is stopping him from being successful.

It is important, as I have said, to keep the aims of the decluttering sessions clear and not to present the person you are helping with too many complex decisions to make. Many hoarders have a tendency not only to overcomplicate a situation but also to create over-elaborate systems. It is essential to keep the process simple and clear, and to steer the person back into focus should she become or appear to be distracted. I find that many people I know who have ADHD and difficulty in focusing benefit from short spurts of processing in one area. However, this can be just as true of anyone – it's easy to become overwhelmed by the clearing process, so if in doubt, start with small sessions (10–15 minutes) and build up.

The use of a kitchen timer can be very productive and helps the person stay focused. Be gentle in guiding her back to the agenda in question and remind her of the purpose of your visit. It is very easy to become preoccupied by a possession if it has only just been rediscovered and evokes memories of times gone by.

Homework

Professionals quite often assign the person they are helping 'homework' or specific tasks to complete. It may be a little condescending to suggest this to the person you are helping if you are a friend or relative, but perhaps you could agree a 'to do' list. It will strengthen the person's ongoing commitment to dealing with his own clutter, and will encourage him to take responsibility and ownership for decluttering and organizing his possessions. Additionally, it helps boost confidence, so that the person increasingly knows that he can continue independently, and use any tools and tips you have provided to help himself. Essentially, providing people with assignments gives them a sense of empowerment and confidence in knowing that they can change their environment. It helps improve motivation and decision-making abilities.

Recently a support worker rang us to express her frustration that her client had not been completing any of the tasks she had set him to reduce his clutter. Our advice to her was to ensure that the tasks were not only mutually agreed, but were also tangible, specific and realistic. In a similar way to a teacher assigning homework at school, you need to ensure that the homework is clearly understood, and that achieving it is a realistic aim.

Some dos and don'ts

If you're helping someone else declutter their home, do:

- imagine yourself in the person's shoes – how would you want to be treated?
- match the person's language – how does she refer to her possessions?
- be guided by the person you are helping;
- use encouraging language;
- be positive about the person's achievements – admire an item that can now be showcased;
- highlight the person's strengths;
- the first things to consider are safety and organization; work on discarding things later;
- be very clear about which items can be recycled and donated, and where;
- always consult with the person as to what he or she would like help with;
- work together and let the person you are helping lead the way;
- keep the momentum going;
- provide lots of encouragement;
- show support and provide reassurance;
- take regular breaks and end the session with an enjoyable activity;
- persist – to a degree. The person you are trying to help might well refuse your offers of help, but continue to offer support;
- be consistent. This will help establish trust and confidence, and as a result the person you are trying to help will be more willing to accept your support;
- work slice by slice, chunk by chunk. Break tasks down into manageable portions.

Don't:

- use judgemental language;
- be negative, or use words that devalue or negatively judge the person's possessions;
- make your own suggestions as to what should be done or where to focus;
- try to persuade or argue;
- touch items without the owner's explicit permission and without being clear about what he or she wants done with that item.

Finally, if you do want to help and support someone who has clutter issues, I would add that you need bagfuls of patience. You also need to be methodical and practical, as well as sensitive and unassuming. From my experience it is essential to have real listening skills, and to resist the temptation to do what you think is right for the person you are helping. Your 'right' might not be their 'right'. You may feel frustrated and baffled by the person you are helping, but it is important to keep your inner voice quiet.

If you are lacking in energy, having a bad day or feeling down and preoccupied by any of your own issues, it's probably best to not transmit this to the person you are helping.

Calling in professional help

In some cases, help from friends and family may not be enough, or the person may prefer to work with someone impartial, on a professional level with no personal implications. The 'Useful addresses' section of this book will give you a few suggestions as to where to start – but make sure any professional declutterer you choose is someone the person you are helping feels comfortable with. Schedule an exploratory session or telephone interview first.

Bear in mind that professional help may entail expert psychological assistance to overcome underlying problems such as anxiety disorder, obsessive–compulsive disorder or depression. In this case, as already suggested, do visit your GP first and get the most appropriate help before tackling the physical manifestations of hoarding.

Personal identity

Many hoarders literally lose themselves within their possessions; their hoard becomes the focus of their life instead of themselves and who they are. Part of our work is to help people retrieve their personal identity, which might involve returning to hobbies they enjoy, activities they want to participate in, or social events they have not felt able to attend. The aim is to help people identify who they are without being preoccupied with their possessions. The book *Stuffocation: Living More with Less*, by James Wallman (Penguin, 2015), describes a healthy life as being one that consists of life experiences and not 'stuff'. Wallman's view that less stuff equates to more happiness, and a richer and more fulfilled life, has been helpful to many hoarders.

Home plans and life skills

Sometimes, people have either forgotten life skills or have neglected to use them in the first place with regard to the maintenance and upkeep of their home. We encourage people to implement systems and solutions that support their own individual needs and are practicable and suitable to their lifestyle and day-to-day living. Clearing the clutter alone is not enough. We need to take a whole, even holistic, approach to the person's life and the way she lives. If we clear the clutter and don't work on the life skills, people tend to continue doing what they have been doing and get the same results, in other words more clutter.

One person we worked with did not recognize the importance of unpacking her bags after a journey out each day. Introducing a discipline of putting things away on her return home each day led to a vastly less cluttered hallway. This is a very simple yet effective example of a home plan.

Life skills play an important part in maintaining an uncluttered environment and we can swiftly establish through our initial assessment whether these skills have been taught, and whether the condition of the home we are working in is the result of the desire to hoard and acquire or whether it is as a result of not being educated in and aware of how to maintain a home. We have been in some homes which, as a direct result of the owner's illness and depression, present as hoarded homes but are in fact a result of chronic overwhelm.

Sorting, organizing and systems

Many of the people I have met are completely overwhelmed by their possessions, and although they think they can organize them, they undoubtedly experience elements of procrastination and fear, among other emotions. Helping someone find systems that work for them and their family means you have to see the world from that person's perspective and try and work out a solution. What works in one home doesn't necessarily work in all homes, so creative thinking is required, as is talking with the person about how they want to use and access the items they need. The systems you put in place should make day-to-day living easier; if the individual tries a different way and finds after a week or so that it doesn't work, then a new solution can be found.

How long will it take?

We are asked this question frequently. There is no set answer. We have worked with both families and individuals to reclaim a space that has become too cluttered in 12–16 weeks, while with others it has taken over 60 weeks. Some people I have known for over three years and continue to touch base with them. Each individual case is different. Factors which affect the length of time the process takes are:

- the size of the home;
- the person's willingness to change;
- any other illnesses or issues involved;
- the person's emotional attachment to particular items;
- the day-to-day challenges that can cause small setbacks;
- the person's ability to work alone;
- the person's commitment to reclaiming space;
- the person's motivation.

It is important not to set time limits, such as 'We will have it all done by Christmas'. Instead, set smaller goals, such as 'Let's aim to have the dining table clear by Christmas'. As hoarding disorder is an anxiety-based disorder, setting fixed timescales can increase the person's anxiety.

Although you may have an idea of what you would like to achieve when you arrive at your friend's or family member's home, it is important to remain focused on the person concerned. Explain where you would like to start, but also ask the person, 'How does that sound?' or 'Do you have any ideas, depending on what has happened since the last session?'

Any change that you can make in a session is a step in the right direction, so praise yourself and congratulate the person. Even if it feels that you are only making baby steps, baby steps are the start of lasting progress.

6

Sustainability – keeping it clear

In this chapter I want to look at how you can help the hoarder to feel empowered, to sustain her efforts and maintain space, including keeping a record of the pace of progress. It is important to celebrate and get used to the reclaimed space. It is so easy to fill the area you have cleared again, so in this chapter I'll also focus on maintaining clear areas.

Capture progress and timelines

Using a progress form which you can create yourself can be useful to measure how far you have come. It is a way to encourage both the person you are helping and yourself – in fact, to motivate all parties concerned, such as friends or family members – and to act as a timeline of the progress achieved.

Many hoarders can quite easily be distracted from the task in hand, so it is essential to recognize how long at a time you can work with the person you are helping. It is important to be mindful of the energy levels both of the person you are helping and your own. We like to conclude our sessions with people still wanting to do more rather than feeling completely exhausted because the sessions have been too arduous, too long and too emotionally challenging. The role of a helper is to instil a sense of enthusiasm and energy in the person you are helping, so that at the end of your session you leave the person feeling motivated, empowered and energized to continue.

Many people can feel despondent and overwhelmed at the scale of their hoard, and it is important to anyone helping to provide reinforcement, encouragement and praise. A written record will highlight just how much has been achieved and which areas have been tackled, where progress has been achieved and clutter-free areas maintained. A progress form not only provides a positive record of achievement for the person but allows friends and helpers to know which areas within the home are being tackled and where best to continue in the next scheduled session. The form can also act as a kind of project management tool, and as a reference guide to the areas of the home that have been addressed on previous sessions.

Aims and gains

Be sure to agree with the person you are helping the areas that you will be focusing on. It is easy to be distracted by areas other than the one you have agreed, and identifying a clear aim provides a clear pathway to ensuring that outcomes can be measured and achieved. Recording aims and gains helps establish realistic goals.

Make sure you celebrate the area that has been cleared, spending some time in it and ensuring that the person feels comfortable with the space. It is also worth re-emphasizing the positive impact that the reclaimed space has made.

What we have achieved

Capturing the progress made within a session is an important way to reaffirm and provide positive feedback. Reinforcement and the reaffirmation of the goals to be achieved is critical to ensuring continuing progress and maintaining the person's commitment to addressing the hoarded home. It is important to focus on the stage you are currently on and not on how many more steps there are still to climb. We cannot stress strongly enough that the key to success in supporting the person in her hoarded home is to work very gently and slowly so that she can adjust to the changes, and have more chance of successfully maintaining that area. A home becomes hoarded over several years, so we cannot then declare that we will make that home a 'house beautiful' with a single dramatic clearout.

The following are some ideas for recording progress:

- Take before and after photos to give a clear visual picture of what's been achieved.
- Be clear about an item's ultimate destination. Use a form to record what the person you are working with has agreed to let go of. It is very important for the person to know the destination of the possessions he or she is letting go of, and knowing that they can be enjoyed and appreciated by those in need can greatly ease the discomfort of letting go. Our support groups echo this belief

and actively share new initiatives, places and causes that need items. Hoarders take great pleasure in knowing that their possessions can be loved and appreciated by those who have little.

- Ensure that the person you are working with is really ready to let go of particular items. One way to do this is to use the 'keep for a week' system described on page 37. Shortly after one man's cat passed away, we helped sort the cat food, the bowls, the scratching pad and other related items during a session. We offered to take them to a local charity shop and thanked the man for the cat food, which was greatly appreciated by one of our volunteers who has a cat. Our client rang a few hours after our visit to say that he had changed his mind and would like the cat bed returned, as he was considering buying a new kitten. We were fortunate enough to be in time to ring the charity shop, and they held it until we could retrieve it.

- Identify items that have strong emotional attachments. In identifying the things that someone is willing to let go of, it's important to highlight those with more emotional resonance – that is, the items to which the person is most emotionally attached. It may well be that the person has strong emotional attachments to things that may have belonged to a loved one who has passed away, or attachments relating to a hobby that he or she can no longer enjoy, or mementos associated with happy times. It is recommended that you do not start in these areas. It is important to start with the items that have the least emotional connotations and build up to the more emotional ones as appropriate, when the person you are working with feels ready to address them.

Tim and Maria

We visited a house owned by Tim and Maria, an older couple whose Christmas decorations were still up and whose house was hung with several calendars that remained open at the month of December. When we asked about the decorations the couple were unable to explain why they were still up; we visited them in June, so there was plenty of time for them to have been taken down. The couple had two daughters, one who lived with Mum and Dad and other who lived away; the daughter who lived away was also unable to explain.

When we eventually spoke to the daughter who lived at home about the decorations, a flood of emotions and tears poured out. It transpired that the family dog had to be put to sleep just before Christmas some five years before, and the family – particularly the live-in daughter – were entrenched in grief over the death of their dog. Their Christmas decorations were still up in memory of the dog and that time of year. The loss of a pet can be just as upsetting as the loss of a relative or friend; we work very closely with Cruse, the bereavement counsellors, who are trained to support people whose beloved pets have passed away.

Tensions, arguments and stress within a cluttered home can run high as a result of the absence of personal space in which to function. It is important to establish and maintain boundaries for communal areas where there are other family members living within a hoarded environment. The following case study may give you some ideas as to how you can help yourself, your friends or family in this respect.

Amanda and Clive

We had been working with a couple, Amanda and Clive, for some time. Amanda approached us for support in clearing her clutter while Clive was away looking after his elderly father. Clive was rather wary of us, as he felt partially to blame for his wife's hoarding and defensive that he had not been able to help her with her clutter. He, like Amanda, had become 'clutter blind' and felt completely overwhelmed as to where to start. After a few sessions with both Amanda and Clive, we were able to provide Amanda with the confidence to make decisions about her hoard and equip Clive with the tools to help support his wife, not only emotionally but from a practical and physical perspective.

They both continue to attend our support group, but have learned through our sessions to use a progress form effectively as a tool for when they declutter together without our help. In fact, they have also gone as far as photographing the items that they are now decluttering. They frequently review their aims and visions to accommodate day-to-day living, issues such as the need to replace white goods, and the adaptations required within their home, but they now feel far more capable of dealing with the daily challenges and recognize that with regular little steps, big changes can be made.

Rules within the home have also been established for the couple, to ensure that both feel they have personal space of their own. One rule, for example, is that possessions do not encroach on a chest of drawers belonging to Clive in the bedroom; another is that the doorway to the spare bedroom is kept clear, in order to continue the process of decluttering all the assorted fabrics that are stored inside.

Staying motivated

As when you are on a diet, motivation can sometimes dwindle when addressing hoarding issues, and a progress form can also be used as part of your reviewing process. The saying 'look how far you have come, not how far you have to go' is particularly pertinent here. When you live in a cluttered environment it is sometimes difficult to view the changes that have been made. A progress form will capture the steps that have been taken and act as proof of what has been achieved to date. By default, negative and self-defeating talk can distract you from the progress you are making, so it is beneficial to review the progress form regularly and to use it as a motivational tool.

Relapses

Continuing review of the various areas of a cluttered home is key to ensuring that progress and the reclaimed space can be maintained. By capturing what is working well, doing it consistently, making time for the process daily, building in and scheduling time to concentrate on maintaining the reclaimed space forms the foundation of maintaining what has been achieved. Small tangible efforts will enable you to go far in achieving the goals you have set. Here are some tips for maintaining progress:

- Build in small changes every day.
- Relish, celebrate and spend time in the space you have cleared.
- Just as if we have had a bad day and binged when we are meant to be slimming, it is easy to be disheartened, but just as easy to get back to good habits.
- Remind the person you are helping to be kind and gentle to herself, and not to be too hard on herself if setbacks occur.
- Recognize that some procrastination is inevitable, and that the tendency may creep back in after an initial spurt of progress. It may be easy to let the pile of newspapers begin to build up again, and you may not get around to dealing with the post as quickly as you should, but acknowledging any avoidance and reluctance will help nip it in the bud here and now.
- Mindfulness works particularly well when a hoarder is feeling defeated and encounters a setback.

7

Where does my stuff go?

It's often very important to people who hoard to know that their treasured possessions will go on to lead a useful life once they leave their owners. This knowledge may even make it easier for some people to let go of their stuff, once they have made the shift from hanging on to it 'in case it's useful one day' to thinking 'maybe someone else can get value from it'. Fortunately, these days, there are many resources for those who would like items to be reused, and who are looking for alternatives to the rubbish tip. This chapter gives information and helpful hints on how to upcycle, recycle, rehome and repurpose the items that are leaving a hoarded house.

It is reassuring to know that when we decide to let go of our stuff, we can do so in the knowledge that it will be enjoyed, used and loved by someone else. When I donate books to charity I always think to myself that I am sharing my reading experience with someone else. The thought of anything going to landfill is upsetting. To some it brings a feeling of being wasteful, frivolous or environmentally unfriendly; to others with strong emotional connections to their things, it brings feelings of disloyalty and abandonment. I am pleased to work with a local charity, Loose Ends, which supports the homeless, and to which many of the people I work with have donated items that include sleeping bags, blankets, coats, food containers and toiletries (the charity is happy to accept half-used toiletries).

Knowing that our possessions can be given a new lease of life is comforting, and it is beneficial to seek out and explore the options available for the destination of your items.

Many members of my hoarding support groups, who live in different boroughs and use different recycling units, wish there was some consistency, a national approach as to how and what recycling units across the country will accept. Ceramics are one example: some counties accept broken ceramics, which are recycled, and this is brilliant when looking at chipped crockery, vases, tiles, toilets, etc. However, in other counties, chipped crockery is disposed of within general rubbish. Perhaps I should make a tour of the tips of England and find out exactly what is recycled, and where . . .

Roger

Roger's house had become very cluttered since the death of his wife Lynn more than five years ago. Lynn had clearly maintained the home and Roger and his son were completely overwhelmed both with the contents of the home and their grief. Lynn had loved knitting and had left behind more than three bin bags of unused wool in pastel shades. Roger was persuaded by his son to part with the bags of wool to a charity that makes blankets for premature babies and for babies in women's refuges. The charity later shared with me photos of the blankets that the volunteers had knitted, and it was heart-warming to show these pictures to Roger.

There are many ways of finding a home for cleared items. Here are just a few examples:

- Any large items, furniture, sports equipment, etc. can be disposed of via Freecycle or free ads in local papers; this is especially useful if you cannot transport the items yourself. There are also local charities and furniture banks for those in need.
- Books can be passed around to friends, family and neighbours, or given to charity shops, sheltered housing libraries or Book Crossing (www.bookcrossing.com).
- Fabric and wool can be given to local charities, WI groups or Brownie groups (any sort of craft supplies).
- Glass can be sent to local recycling depositories or charity shops.

What can be recycled?

Below is a list of items that can generally be recycled:

- batteries
- books
- bricks
- cans
- car batteries
- cardboard
- clothing

- computers
- electricals (even broken ones)
- engine oil
- fluorescent lighting tubes
- foil
- food waste
- furniture
- garden waste
- glass
- mobile phones
- paint
- paper
- plastic bags
- plastic bottles
- shoes
- soil
- spectacles
- tins
- toner and printer cartridges
- water filters

There may be other items in addition to those listed – check with your local council if you are in doubt about specific items. Other resources for recycling are suggested below.

Animal shelters

Many animal shelters, such as the Dogs Trust and Cats Protection, are keen to receive blankets and towels for the animals in their care. They also accept many other donations, selling the items to support their cause.

Schools

It is always a good idea to enquire whether your local schools need any items. One gentleman who was downsizing from a three-bedroom house to a one-bedroom flat needed to be quite specific about his collections. We worked to donate his complete musical collection of rain sticks, flutes, recorders, tambourines and a guitar to a local special needs school where music was a key element of the curriculum.

Overseas charities

Many initiatives need items of clothing, including underwear and shoes, as well as notebooks, pens and pencils to send to support overseas communities. Other items required range from broken lawnmowers to old car engines.

Hospitals, hospices, care homes and churches

It is best to check with individual organizations which donations are wanted – items that are commonly required range from books and blankets to jigsaw puzzles and DVDs. One great initiative I have come across is that some hospitals welcome foreign currency and have collection points at which to donate foreign coins and notes.

Food banks

Many supermarkets have an area for donations of food, which can be distributed to people in need either locally or internationally. They generally require items such as tinned meat, fish and fruit, cereals, pasta and rice.

Specific charities

The following list comprises charities to which I have donated items; apologies for any I may have missed out.

- Age UK
- British Heart Foundation – collections available
- Barnardo's
- British Red Cross
- Cancer Research
- Community Furniture Project – collections available
- Marie Curie
- Mind
- Oxfam
- RSPCA
- Salvation Army
- Scope
- Shelter
- Sue Ryder

I have intentionally not listed the items each of the above charities accepts, as this frequently changes based on what is needed locally.

Some charities accept furniture, electrical and other household goods, most accept bric-a-brac, clothes, handbags, unopened toiletries, towels, curtains, bedding, children's toys, CDS, DVDs, shoes, artwork, records, crockery, cutlery and glasses. But it is always best to check in advance what your local charities are accepting.

I have been fortunate enough to meet Mary Herbert, who is involved with a group of women who call themselves Pins and Needles and who knit and sew in north-west Hampshire. Mary describes the group as being mainly of an age that remember clothing coupons and ration books and who have sewing machines and needles in their cupboards. The ladies make fabric 'fiddle blankets' and knitted 'fiddle muffs' and work alongside the Alzheimer's Society ('fiddle', 'busy' or activity blankets have been shown to help restless hands and minds, helping soothe stress and discomfort in people with dementia, as well as in patients in rehab or after an operation). A volunteer came to one of my support groups to show us what a fiddle blanket looks like and to show how the donations she has received from us at Hoarding Disorders UK – including fabric, zips, whistles, wool, ribbons and buttons – have been used. This is a wonderful initiative and a cause many people I know are keen to support. The charity also makes personal bags for our local palliative care teams and angel blankets for stillborn babies.

The condition of items

We may worry that we haven't ironed a piece of clothing that is destined for the charity shop. It is worth knowing that charity shops use a steamer to deal with creasing and to eradicate any lingering odours on items of clothing. If the clothing is not deemed saleable on the shop floor, the charity can decide that the items will either be ragged or used as stuffing for furniture.

Auctioneers

It is really useful to invest some time in researching local auction houses and find out what they are happy to try and sell on your behalf. Many auctioneers are interested in 'retro' items and unusual collections. Vinyl records are very popular at the time of writing, and there are record specialists and book specialists who will meet with you and view your collection.

Dress agencies

You may well have vintage clothes that you would like to make some money for you, and expensive clothes that no longer suit you. Using a dress agency is a useful avenue for this. Always check with the agency as to what they are willing to accept. For example, some agencies accept wedding dresses and fur coats, while others don't.

Car boot sales

Having a car boot sale or garage sale is another way of selling your possessions. Be prepared however for cheeky offers. Having once been very offended to be offered just 20p for a top that cost me over £15 and used to be a firm favourite, though it no longer fitted me, I learned that it is probably not a good idea to try and use a car boot sale to sell anything of sentimental value. Always have a Plan B for items that you don't sell – perhaps that they will remain in your car for a trip to the charity shops.

Online resources

There are several online resources for getting rid of stuff, but these can sometimes pose difficulties for people who hoard; the sales process is often longer and more involved than a quick trip to the charity shop, or a collection from home. The business of posting ads and pictures, and of arranging for collection, or of wrapping objects to take to the post office, can sometimes be daunting, as well as giving people time to change their minds about letting go of something! So a hoarder might need help and support through the selling process until he becomes accustomed to it. This is particularly true of some older people, who may not be familiar with the internet. This said, there are some great resources, such as Freecycle, to help clear space and even make a little money. See 'Useful addresses' for details – or try googling 'Sell my stuff online' and add 'local' for nearby schemes.

And finally . . .

You don't always *have* to find a good home for every single item you want to dispose of! Sometimes it's not worth the time and energy you may spend deciding on the perfect location, and you may just have to trust your decision to let an item go. In this case you can:

- Make an act of trust and give items to a friend to dispose of.
- Take them to the charity shop without being quite sure they are useful, and trust the charity shop to pass them on to the right destination.
- Simply put them out with the rubbish.
- Leave them in an open carrier bag by the rubbish so a passer-by can take them if he or she wishes.
- Leave larger items, e.g. furniture, outside the house. One woman left a new, wrapped mattress (her father had died before he could use it), a bed frame and a chest of drawers outside her house – they had all gone within half an hour.

Although this isn't recommended, some people just leave items in bags besides recycling points, as a kind of hopeful, informal donation to whoever wants it.

8

Helpful therapies

We quite often come across individuals and professionals who do not know where to turn to access information, advice, guidance and support to help with hoarding issues, be it in terms of understanding, providing practical support, or both.

The NHS website recommends that the first point of contact should be your GP, so do consider making an appointment to see your doctor. There are therapies, support groups, decluttering services, websites and Facebook groups, all of which can help with hoarding. It's very important to select an organization, therapy or person that can help and not hinder, and who offers a person-centred approach.

Counselling can be of value in addressing any underlying issues that need to be straightened out before a house can be cleared – as the saying goes, the situation is within the person, rather than within the house. As we have seen, sometimes clutter can represent anger, grief, stress, feelings of inner disorganization or loss, or of low self-worth. Bereavement counselling can be particularly helpful when hoarding is triggered by loss – for example, when the death of one or both parents leaves the person with all their worldly goods to sort out. I have seen many hoarded homes where the person was struggling with belongings inherited from both parents as well as a lifetime of their own accumulated possessions, often because they could not face or deal with their grief at losing their parents.

Exposure therapy, used for people with OCD, may also help some people with hoarding disorder, depending on their individual underlying uses.

Cognitive Behavioural Therapy (CBT)

CBT is a behavioural therapy and helps to change the way that we think and behave. It is generally used to treat depression, PTSD, phobias, OCD, anxiety, feelings of overwhelm and other mental health issues. It can help with hoarding behaviours too. CBT deals with the 'now' rather than focusing on issues of the past, and looks at practical ways to help with the daily challenges we experience. The aim of CBT is to ultimately teach you skills that you can apply to your daily life – from changes in shopping habits to the way we think, feel and behave. CBT involves a change of mindset and confronting your emotions and anxieties.

The advantages of CBT are that it can be helpful alongside other support systems and by its nature can be provided in a variety of forms, whether a therapy setting, group settings or self-help books. In our hoarding support groups we have used some CBT exercises from the book *Overcoming Hoarding*, a self-help guide by Satwant Singh, Margaret Hooper and Colin Jones that uses cognitive behavioural techniques (see 'Further reading'). We strongly recommend this book. Many of those attending support groups have benefited from reading it.

Not everyone, however, can benefit from CBT. It requires the cognitive part of your brain to work, which means that it may not be suitable for anyone experiencing more complex mental health issues, or people with learning difficulties or on the autistic spectrum. CBT involves looking at and questioning our feelings and actions, and aims to change thought patterns which can be self-defeating and negative. Some of the disadvantages of CBT are that it can evoke uncomfortable feelings, leave you feeling anxious and stir up emotions that you find difficult to confront.

We would recommend that you visit your GP to establish whether or not CBT is a recommended route for assisting with hoarding issues for yourself or someone you know.

Peter: a case history of CBT

Peter believed that his difficulties with having too many things, or not being able to discard things, started after a close relative died and his mother committed suicide. Sadly, such traumatic events do sometimes underlie hoarding behaviours.

Peter had been having CBT for depression, and the house was full (the Clutter Image Rating downstairs was 8/9 on the scale) of things like designer clothes (still with the labels on), shoes, luggage and technology (laptops, printers, mobile phones and other gadgets). He bought and wore new clothes because he couldn't access the washing machine, and liked technology because 'it couldn't hurt him'.

He slept in his bedroom. Other than the hallway, which could accommodate one person at a time, this was the only room in the house that could just about be accessed – and was the place where he spent most of his time when he was at home. The switch for the landing light was inaccessible due to the piles of clutter, so he wore a head lamp in order to see when he scrambled upstairs like a mountain goat, often causing avalanches. The bathroom was unusable so he showered at the gym.

What convinced him to make a start at getting help to clear the house and reclaim his home was CBT. Although his view is that CBT doesn't work for everyone, and that it also depends on the practitioner, it helped Peter recognize that his hoarding had become a habit, and come to the conclusion that the habit needed to be broken, through baby steps.

Several years down the line, the house is a home to him and his two beloved dogs ('more of a dog-den than a stereotypical home') – 'the best treatment I have experienced since it all came to the surface'.

He says that his depression continues and 'I'm not out of the woods yet . . . all is not perfect', although to the outside world, most would never know.

For more information on CBT please visit the NHS Choices website, or to access a therapist contact the British Association for Behavioural & Cognitive Psychotherapies (BABCP), which keeps a register of all accredited therapists in the UK, or the British Psychological Society (BPS), which has a directory of psychologists who specialize in CBT (see 'Useful addresses').

Emotional Freedom Technique (EFT)

EFT, also known as 'tapping', is a healing method designed to boost mental health. A simple yet powerful way of releasing emotions from your mind and body, it involves lightly drumming your fingertips on various parts of your head and body, while repeating key sentences and affirmations that focus on the issues you wish to address. It's believed that this helps release stuck negative emotions and behaviours, allowing the person to move on. In addition to helping people with hoarding disorder, EFT has been used to help with a range of problems such as fears, phobias, addictions including compulsive eating, self-sabotaging behaviour patterns, trauma, depression and OCD.

How does it work? Tapping is usually described as a fingertip form of acupressure, accessing energy points below the skin around the body. Alternatively, some people believe that using this physical cue, and addressing problems in a focused, specific way, together with the use of positive affirmations, makes us more aware of those problems, and helps us to use mind power to overcome them. You could say that you are almost literally tapping into the power of your subconscious to help change unwelcome behaviours and habits!

When Amanda Peet and I started Hoarding Disorders UK, together we evolved various therapies to try and help hoarders. As part of this, Amanda trained as an EFT practitioner. She has found tapping to be invaluable in getting your 'life back on track' and has helped people who have experienced severe trauma in their life which has held them back.

The internal chatter that drives you mad, the rise of heat in your body when something untoward happens or someone says something that triggers off unhappy emotions, can all be effectively soothed and managed with EFT. Most of us will probably know what our triggers are, those events that annoy us or send us down like a lead balloon from a happy, perky mood until we feel as if we are in a pit of despair. Sometimes, an incident from the past, or a few words casually dropped by someone and not meant to harm, can really hurt your feelings and change your mood for the rest of the day. Sometimes, such encounters can change you for the rest of your life.

Between birth and the age of six we are like sponges, and this is when we experience emotions for the first time. It is also when we work out how to deal with those emotions. Parents who are aware of their children's emotional well-being are easily able to see the world through their eyes and to provide relevant support. Parents who have a great deal going on in their own lives, and who are themselves less able to cope with adult life, will find it more difficult. Without support and guidance to understand what our emotions are doing to us, as little people we work out our own strategies for dealing with them, and since those strategies work for us, we then tend to stick with them right the way through to adulthood unless they are questioned or an event happens that forces us to adjust our strategies.

We all experience emotions every day, lots and lots of them. We all have a level. Imagine a spirit level. When it is flat and the bubble is in the middle, this is our level. Lift it up and the bubble moves; move it down and again the bubble moves. Imagine that the bubble represents your emotions. After you experience positive emotions, the bubble will come back to your level. We don't hold on to positive emotions and stay in that excited, happy mode for ever – we can't, we would never sleep! So we go back to our calm level with the bubble in the middle. Emotions can be positive like happiness, joy and excitement, or negative like sadness, anger or despair. Positive emotions come and they last for a time, and then we are back to our level. Negative emotions tip our level down but make it somehow harder to get back to our level. Events in your past, and your life story, can sometimes make it harder to come back to your level after experiencing negative emotions.

Our brains act like a search engine. Here is an example: suppose you are going about your day and come across an item in your house that stirs up a negative emotion. It might be that you find a pet toy after your pet has passed away and is no longer with you. This can make you feel all sorts of emotions, but let's say it makes you feel sad and then guilty – sad because your pet has gone and guilty because you feel that you should have done more for it. Maybe you were the one who had to take a sick animal to the vet to help ease its pain and let it pass away with dignity – you may be feeling guilt for that.

Your brain recognizes and registers the sadness and guilt you are feeling in that moment, and you think, 'Ah OK, I am feeling this.' Your brain then goes into search-engine mode and starts spinning through all your memories, sending you the emotional intensity of all the times you have ever felt sad or guilty. In other words, you experience not just the present event, but a whole layer of old memories as well, as if they had only just happened. Naturally this can be overwhelming, and it may stop you in your tracks. In turn it can bring on a panic attack, as a result of which you feel that you can't go on with your day as you had planned. You get stuck.

EFT can help you make sense of your emotions, and why you are feeling the way you do. It also helps remove the intensity of emotions brought up by past events, so that as and when those feelings crop up again, your head is clearer, and when your brain tries to google those events and triggers, they have been dealt with, so they can no longer bring up such a level of intensity in you. You no longer have to spin through a host of old emotions; you can simply deal with the emotion in that moment, linked to whatever is going on at that time.

What does EFT involve?

If you are doing EFT with a practitioner you sit opposite the prac-titioner. If you using it via YouTube, again you sit opposite the screen. The practitioner, either virtual or in person, will tap various points around their face and body. As they are tapping, they will speak and leave time for you to copy the points they are tapping and repeat what they are saying.

The tapping points are the same points that an acupuncturist would use, but instead of using needles on the points, you are using your fingers to tap, gently and repeatedly, anything from 4 to 10 times. The tapping points are as follows, and are illustrated in Figure 2 overleaf (you can use either hand and either side of your face, whichever is more comfortable for you):

- karate chop – side of the hand, below your little finger
- above the eye – on the inside corner of your eyebrow
- side of the eye – the side of your head between the outside of your eye and your hairline
- below the eye – where those bags are
- under the nose, the area below your nose and above your top lip
- under the mouth, between your bottom lip and your chin
- collarbone – the part in the centre where the knot of a man's tie would be
- under the arm or the inside of the wrist. Some people find it difficult to tap under their arm, the part under your armpit where a woman's bra would sit, so an alternative is the inside of your wrist
- the top of the head in the centre.

Work out which emotion you want to deal with and then rate its intensity from 0 to 10, 0 being nothing at all and 10 the worst ever. As you tap, repeat sentences that refer to the emotions you are making sense of: accept the emotion, acknowledge where it came from, and release it when you feel safe to do so.

What follows is a tapping script to give you an idea. This is only very brief and general, because we all feel emotions for many different reasons. No two lives are the same, and although we may have experienced the same life event, such as dealing with the death of a family member, the circumstances and other factors surrounding it will be unique to you. So I would advise you always to use a practitioner to address the more complex issues. Then, as you become more confident with EFT, you will be able to do it yourself. Most sessions take around an hour and afterwards you are likely to feel quite drained. After all, something you have been carrying for 10, 20, 30 or more years has been released, and you may well feel

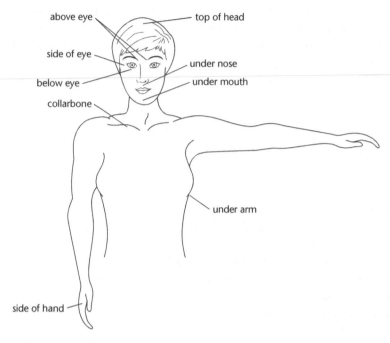

above eye
top of head
side of eye
under nose
below eye
under mouth
collarbone
under arm
side of hand

Figure 2 Tapping points

different physically, so make sure you are kind to yourself and allow yourself time to rest after an EFT session.

There are many different techniques that can be used with EFT. I am explaining the basic technique here. It is a bit like having a recipe. There is a set-up statement which you say while tapping the karate chop point, repeating it three times before going into the other points. So here's the taster . . .

Tapping for overwhelm

The emotion we are working on is overwhelm.

1 Ask yourself how much overwhelm you are feeling. Give it a score between 0 and 10, where 0 is none and 10 is the worst ever, and write this down.
2 Karate chop point with side of hand – repeat three times. As you tap, repeat, 'Even though I feel completely overwhelmed and I don't know where to start, I am learning to accept myself.'
3 Then tap through:
   • above the eye: *All this overwhelm*
   • side of the eye: *All this overwhelm*

- below the eye: *It's just so difficult*
- under the nose: *I don't know where to start*
- under the mouth: *I don't know what to do, so I end up doing nothing*
- collarbone: *All this overwhelm*
- under arm or inside wrist: *All this overwhelm*
- top of the head: *I am open to the possibility*
- above the eye: *That this funny tapping thing might be able to help*
- side of the eye: *It has helped other people*
- below the eye: *So it might work for me*
- under the nose: *I do feel a bit silly*
- under the mouth: *but if it gets rid of these intense emotions, I'll try anything!*
- collarbone: *All this overwhelm*
- under arm or inside wrist: *I'd like to release some of it to see how it feels*
- top of the head: *Releasing this overwhelm through my body and mind.*

Take a deep breath, and see how it feels. Now, again grade your feelings by writing down a number between 0 and 10. The number may have gone up or down, or stayed the same. Then repeat if you want to. I hope this sample of tapping will get you started (see 'Useful addresses' for EFT websites).

Bear in mind that the therapeutic effect isn't limited to the current moment, but can filter through and have a positive effect in general. Emotions are not restricted to particular areas of our lives, so if you deal with an emotion from one event, the benefits are likely to be felt in your life overall.

Our experience has shown that EFT works particularly well with people who hoard. It can also help their families. Research into effective interventions for people with hoarding disorder is still in its early days, but some experts have called for EFT to be an area that should be further explored. Staffordshire University is leading research into the effectiveness of EFT as an intervention that might help a wide range of conditions.

Although there were many emotions involved in the following case, I am going to focus on just one.

The angry family
We were helping a family where the mother was affected by hoarding disorder and was angry because everyone was trying to get her to throw her things out. The father meanwhile was angry because Mother wasn't

sorting things out; their daughter was angry because she didn't feel loved or wanted; and their son was angry, but he stayed in his room a lot. Mother wouldn't do EFT one to one, but agreed to try it in order to help her daughter. So the mother, daughter and father tapped together. We tapped on anger, and they all started with high numbers, 8, 9 and 10, which we slowly managed to reduce.

The father explained that he had realized where his anger came from, and we then tried some one-to-one EFT. This helped enormously. He still felt angry, but his anger wasn't the great anger fuelled by past events any more. It felt different and he was able to manage things a bit better in the short term, until the house got sorted out and the mother changed her collecting behaviours.

The mother had her own reasons for collecting, which came from life events during childhood. As a child she had had to create her own strategies in response to negative emotions to keep herself safe. She couldn't talk to anyone about it, so as an adult in her forties she was responding to emotions through the eyes of a five-year-old.

Here is another example of how complex our emotions are, and how they may be deeply interlinked with our homes and the things we have in them.

Sandra

Sandra was struggling to throw away out-of-date food. She didn't want to get rid of it because she didn't like waste, and she thought that the food was safe and healthy to hang on to. We started with a small cupboard in the top of a dresser which was full of jams and chutneys. To start with, we worked using a rule that if it was out of date then we would consider throwing it away. I checked each label, read the date out loud and passed it to Sandra. At first she agreed to throw away almost every item; the chutneys were a little more challenging because they were pickled, but even they had seen better days. Eventually we had cleared the cupboard and there were only a few items to go back into it, although before we did this it was important for Sandra to tell us how she felt seeing the small empty space.

Suddenly there was a surge of emotion and Sandra felt panicky. We started tapping on the collarbone until she calmed down a little and was able to tell me how she felt. Sandra said she felt empty and lonely, and as I could see she was distressed I didn't press her for more detail – we just started to tap on how she felt. 'Even though I feel empty when I see empty spaces, even though . . .' We tapped for around an hour or so, and the life events that had made Sandra feel this way raised themselves from her subconscious as she felt safe to let them do so. Sandra was able to release all sorts of emotions, including those relating to the loss of a baby, the loss of her brother and mother, and the death of another dear friend. Miscarriage grief is something that not all mothers or would-be mothers deal with. It is one of those subjects where nobody really knows what to say to you; people therefore often say nothing, so that no sense can be made of such a sad situation. For Sandra, a miscarriage compounded with all the other losses in her life had made things increasingly difficult.

EFT on YouTube

There are many videos about EFT on YouTube. For the most part they are not specifically to do with hoarding, but they are geared to specific emotions, so if you can identify the emotion you are feeling, you can probably find a tap-along that suits you. My own favourites include:

- Brad Yates (powerful and humorous)
- Pamela Bruner
- Margaret Lynch
- Nick and Jessica Ortner

Good words to search for are EFT, Tapping.

Please take full responsibility for your well-being if you choose to do EFT. If you are looking for a therapist, many qualified practitioners can be found on <www.aamet.org>.

Mindfulness

With so many mindfulness colouring books clogging the magazine racks in supermarkets and displayed so prettily on the tables in bookshops, I felt I must find out more about this phenomenon. I was fortunate enough through a women's networking event to meet Sheila Bond. Sheila retired as a physiotherapist from the NHS a few years ago and is now a mindfulness coach. She explained to me the benefits of mindfulness, which I also like to call 'remembering', and I eagerly signed up for her eight-week course.

Mindfulness is a warm and gentle therapy that helps increase our awareness of our thoughts, feelings, body sensations and the physical world around us at this present time. It may involve listening to the chirping of the red robins as we wake, being aware of the crispness of our ironed shirt, or enjoying the smell of percolated coffee and the glory of the sky. Mindfulness reminds us not to get caught up in our thoughts and allows us to stand back from our thoughts, to realize that they are just thoughts, and to start to see a pattern in them.

How can mindfulness help with hoarding? Mindfulness provides us with a licence to free ourselves from our past, to stop worrying about the future and concentrate on the present. It allows us to breathe and relax, and provides tools to help deal with our anxious thoughts. Hoarding, as we know, is an anxiety-based disorder, and letting go of our thoughts and slowing down helps us accept the difficult and uncomfortable experiences that may underlie anxiety, while enabling us to appreciate the lovely and happy ones. It helps us to train ourselves to notice when our thoughts are taking over and realize that we have control over those thoughts. It allows us to be kind to ourselves and helps manage self-criticism. It helps us to collect moments and not things, and reminds us of the need for gratitude and appreciation. There are many breathing and meditation exercises you can access.

Mindfulness is now taught in schools, and mindfulness training is becoming popular in the corporate world to help improve both productivity and self-awareness. It is taught in prisons to reduce friction among inmates and increase self-esteem. For further information on how to access a mindfulness course please visit <www.breathworks-mindfulness.org.uk>.

You might also be interested in the Sheldon Press series of mindfulness books, The Mindful Way. The topics covered include anxiety, depression, quitting smoking, pain management and keeping a journal, which deals with writing and creativity.

Support groups

We hold two hoarding support groups, which run monthly and include coaching and therapies. We have invited speakers to talk about topics such as stress management, talking therapies, bereavement counselling, money management, and improving confidence in public speaking. Additionally, we use the sessions to complete and discuss cognitive behavioural techniques (see page 66). Feedback on these exercises has been very positive.

As part of the outreach work carried out by the local Watermill Theatre, our hoarding support group in Newbury were asked to contribute to the composition of a poem for their open workshop 'Our Untold Stories'. We were thrilled with the result and it vividly captures the thoughts and frustrations of living in a hoarded house. The poem is in their own words, composed from the answers to various questions – some negative and some positive – about how our members feel about their homes, hoarding and clutter.

Seeing carpet
Overwhelming, never-ending
Expensive, isolating
Lonely, excluding
Hefty, frustrating
Everywhere, time-consuming
A drain on your energies
No one else in the world understands this loneliest place on
    earth
My house held hostage to a shopaholic gone mad who buys and
    buys and buys and buys
Trapped in your head and trapped in your home
A punishment for an unknown crime
An enormous, heavy secret
You try to run away from all the time but you can't
A magnet that draws you back
But you keep going
Taking baby steps
Towards decluttering one room
Towards having a decluttered home
Taking the first two big steps, admitting the problem and doing
    something about it
Clearing, and maintaining, some clear space
Finding your MOT certificate
Celebrating feeling able to invite people over
Being able to have family sat at the table
Being able to sleep in my bed
Going shopping and not buying anything you don't need
Not worrying about where you're going to put the shopping
    down
And when you put something down it stays there
Not feeling dread when you turn the key to go back into your
    home
Knowing there are no avalanches waiting
Knowing that there is a home for everything and everything is
    in its home
Knowing you're not alone
Success is seeing carpet

9

The professionals' perspective

A variety of professionals may be involved in tackling hoarding. Some are volunteers, working with organizations like ours or with charities. In more serious cases, social workers or personnel from environmental health may be involved. I sincerely hope you or your loved ones never need the help of the fire brigade, but they provide invaluable assistance and advice in preventing hoarding-related accidents. This chapter looks at hoarding from the perspective of the professionals, and makes it clear what a difficult and delicate path they sometimes have to tread in more complex cases of hoarding.

The volunteer

We often have volunteers helping us out in cluttered homes. One of our volunteers here shares her story and her own perspective on clearing. She also shares her experience and reflections on how it 'used to be done' when she was employed by a local authority.

> 'Why do you want to spend your free time clearing out old people's filthy houses?' I am often asked. Well, that's two myths about people with hoarding difficulties – they are not always old and quite often not filthy. The diverse range of people falling into the category of hoarders is what makes working with them fascinating and very worthwhile, particularly when you can see them turn the corner, manage their hoarding and begin to enjoy having their living space back.
>
> Working as a volunteer with Hoarding Disorders UK could be seen as bit of a busman's holiday for me as I had spent over 20 years as an Environmental Health Officer (EHO) with the local authority before taking early retirement.
>
> Hoarding and hoarders have been part of my personal life too. My aunt, who was only three years older than me, has been a hard-core hoarder for as long as I can remember. It had always fascinated me why she should choose to live the way she did when her sister, my mother, was just the opposite, being fastidious about cleanliness and tidiness.

My mother was the eldest, with a younger brother. Tragically, he died in a drowning accident when he was only nine years old. My grandparents had another child essentially to replace their loss: my aunt. Of course she was never going to take his place, and it appears she had a rather difficult childhood as a result. She was very bright and artistic but was denied the opportunity to go to college until she left home at 18. She took comfort in books and magazines, in fact any reading material, and this very quickly got out of control. She fell into one of the recognized hoarding categories: those with a difficult upbringing, triggering a need to literally surround herself with her possessions to the point of being unable to use her space for its intended purpose. When she was still quite young her home was at 9 on the Clutter Image Rating. At the time, hoarding was not seen as a mental disorder, and I am sure all the family and neighbours felt she just needed to have a good tidy up and perhaps had suffered from a lack of maternal guidance on good housekeeping. This of course was not the case.

My aunt continues to live in her own home, not inviting anyone in and being staunchly independent and private, and I suspect the house still has a CIR of 9. But she now has a PhD and is very active in her community teaching English as a second language. As family we have long backed off trying to help, but we are safe in the knowledge that she knows we understand her need to be allowed to continue to live as she chooses, as long as her circumstances do not impinge on anyone else, and that we are there when she needs help.

This fascination gave me a head start when my career took a turn away from the water quality issues I had been employed to undertake, to those of environmental nuisance and housing conditions. The two tend to go hand in hand. The first the local authority knows about a hoarder is normally when they are alerted by neighbours who may be suffering from pests (flies, rats and mice), an unkempt garden or perhaps housing disrepair. Social workers may find working with such people impossible due to their cluttered surroundings; housing officers may be at a loss as to how to cope with hoarding tenants.

Environmental Health Officers operate within a framework of legislation. Various pieces of legislation allow the EHO to determine whether formal action is necessary to achieve an improvement in the living conditions of the hoarder that may be having an impact on others. They are very often called in as a last resort and many a meeting of professionals looks to the EHO to break the stalemate which can occur in knowing where to turn next. The action taken is often seen as draconian; clearing a home against the will of the occupant is not taken lightly and will undoubtedly cause the occupant some considerable stress, which needs to be managed. EHOs will have sleepless nights too, reflecting on whether they have made the right decision. It is very much a case of 'damned if you do and damned if you don't'.

To illustrate this, I shall reflect briefly on two cases I dealt with during my career. The first was that of an elderly woman living in a detached bungalow. The local authority was alerted to the state of the property by neighbours. The quite considerable garden area was very overgrown, and was infested with rats. The occupier was clearly a hoarder and her hoarding extended to keeping milk bottles of urine all around the outside of the house. She threw nothing away and was paranoid about anything personal being put out in the rubbish. Not only did she keep everything, in fact, she collected useful items from the bins in town and was well known in the area as a Mr Trebus. (Edmund Zygfryd Trebus was a compulsive hoarder, originally from Poland, who was featured on the British television documentary series *A Life of Grime*.)

We had an obligation to the neighbours to deal with the rat population, which we did regularly, and we built up a close relationship with the woman. However, although we knew the house was full of possessions, and particularly newspapers (we could see the tunnels she had made through the newspapers from the limited opening at the front door), we had no authority to insist legally on a clearout as the internal condition of the house was affecting no one but the owner. We did, however, try and persuade her to allow us in to offer some help. This was very forcefully declined, as it had been when her family had tried previously.

The case ended in tragedy. I was called late one afternoon by the fire brigade, who understood we had some contact with the owner of a property that was ablaze. They were not sure if the owner was at home when the blaze started and were instigating a search of the town. Members of my team helped in that search until late in the night, such was their involvement in the case. Sadly, the woman was at home and died in the blaze, as we had predicted a few years earlier. A lot of 'if only' questions were asked in the following weeks and months.

The second case was similar but involved a house attached to its neighbour by a garage. It involved a classic hard-core hoarder couple who felt everything had a use, and 45 years of throwing nothing away had led to disrepair beyond anything we had seen. While we carefully engaged the husband in trying to access the premises his wife was taken ill, and it took several emergency workers hours to get her out; they had to break down the front door and dig their way into the lounge where she was. When, sadly, she died five days later, her husband accused us of killing her.

He was left alone and unable to cope, and we were alerted by a social worker some 18 months later. This time we took swift – some would say drastic – measures to clear his house to allow grant-aided repairs to be carried out. He was rehoused for the duration in respite care. Conditions inside the house were very poor due to a lifetime of neglect. Not only was the property filled with assorted clutter, but the external vegetation on the front wall had broken through the windows to a thickness of about three feet inside, and ivy was even growing through the TV. The disrepair was so bad that the estimates exceeded any grant aid available and the premises lay empty for much longer than we had hoped.

The shock of finding his home cleared and the repairs delayed for so long was too much for the widower and he remained in respite care. At first he was very angry and resentful of our involvement, but over time he came to realize he was now being looked after and, when he died over a year later, it was with some dignity in warm and safe surroundings. I had reservations at the outset about the course of action we had taken, but ultimately he did not suffer or die alone in a cold and cluttered property where he may not have been found for weeks.

Where was the council? was the cry in both cases, but when the local authority did step in, the cry was, How could they do that to an old man? As I said, damned if you do and damned if you don't.

With ever-shrinking local authority budgets, the time available to the EHO to spend cajoling and persuading hoarders is now very limited. Gone are the days when an EHO could spend time getting to know her client; decisions have to be made and action initiated quickly. This action will be a one-off 'hit' – clear up and leave. In my experience, this is a very short-term solution. I am not sure whether the high costs, both monetary and emotional, of house clearance are justified. Could that money be better spent on giving time to other professionals working with people with hoarding difficulties to achieve a long-term solution?

With this background, I turned to volunteering a year after I left the local authority. The hoarders haven't changed, but my approach has. Gone is the legislative framework which dictated my course of action. Hoarding Disorders UK allows me the freedom to work with individuals, so I can help them manage their hoarding. Yes, there is an element of house clearance, but it is done with the full co-operation of the person concerned, and will hopefully lead to the long-term change in behaviour we seek. I have the luxury of more time now.

So which approach do I favour? Well, obviously, the gentler approach causes much less stress and can eventually lead to people managing their space more efficiently, but I still advocate that the EHO has a part to play in dealing with chronic hoarders. If others are suffering as a result of someone's hoarding tendencies, then immediate action may be the only answer. Many cases, including that of my own family, are not easy to deal with and there is often a resistance that cannot be overcome without the help of the law.

In one case during my local authority days the people involved showed more resistance than I had seen for a long while, with elements of aggression, greed, filth and pure laziness. Using the law was the only way the neighbours could be given any respite from the rats, flies and external rubbish that had plagued them for so many years. It was probably the only case of hoarding where I felt no sympathy with the occupants.

The couple in question lived in absolute squalor. They were in their seventies and, I imagine, had lived like this for many years. They had family, but it was clear they had lost contact with them over the years. They were intent on fighting any authority, threatening to sue for poor treatment at the drop of a hat. Their claims against the local ambulance service, the local authority and the police were all unfounded, but caused professionals many hours' work defending themselves against spurious accusations.

Ultimately the EHO was called in. The terraced property was unkempt to the front and like a rubbish tip to the rear, with a large infestation of rats. The power had been cut off, so the inside was dark; the house was damp due to a water leak and cluttered to a CIR level of about 7, mainly with thousands of cassette tapes and videos. The husband and wife were dirty themselves and the wife was in very poor health, with a chest infection. It was winter and the temperature outside was below freezing.

In the kitchen we found layers of greasy filth on every surface. The refrigerator had to be prised open. Inside, the contents were so mouldy that several hardened professionals were sent scurrying for fresh air! The husband at this point wanted compensation for the loss of a beef joint he claimed was in there, such was his deluded grip on reality.

We visited three at a time because of the threats and aggression shown by both parties. We had no choice but to serve notices and insti-gate a clear-up. While this took place the wife lived in the rubbish-filled car outside. The husband was verbally and physically aggressive to both the local authority workers and the clearance personnel, and at one point the police were called to maintain order.

Eventually the property was cleared and the outside made free of pests, but sadly the wife was admitted to hospital from the car and died of pneumonia shortly afterwards. The husband remained in the property for another year before he too passed away.

No matter what the approach, the bottom line is money; someone ultimately has to pay. My time may come without cost, but the service cannot run totally cost free. Getting a hoarder to change his or her behaviour is a long process, and it may be months or even years before any noticeable improvement is seen. If the housing conditions are having a detrimental impact on those around the hoarder, then legislation may need to be used to give professionals a chance to work with the person. There is a need to balance everyone's expectations in severe cases.

Many professionals regularly come into contact with hoarders, but until recently they had no idea where to go for help. Providing housing officers, social workers and health professionals with information on the signs to be aware of and the options open to them is a start. One person's clutter and filth is another person's untidiness, and having common guidance to which to refer, such as the Clutter Image Rating, is a big step forward.

Giving regular updates on cases and their outcomes is also good practice. Hoarding liaison groups, bringing together all the professionals in an area, can inform the process and save a lot of wasted time. These groups tend to work best if everyone buys into the process and, within the bounds of confidentiality, commits to sharing information.

One thing is clear to me. Having been on both sides of the fence, education of the professionals involved and communication on cases is key. The sooner a hoarder is identified, the more likelihood there is that his behaviour can be changed and the correct help engaged – and the help, once it is there, kept on track.

Don't support the disorder, support the individual – a support coordinator's perspective on hoarding

As part of her research into hoarding, Jay Gathergood has used semi-structured interviews to investigate how people who hoard regulate their emotions. She has attended hoarding support groups and is keen to highlight the importance of empowering individuals to make their own choices.

In my line of work, the term 'person-centred support' gets thrown around a lot, but it isn't until you have worked with people who have been institutionalized their whole life that the importance of this paradigm becomes apparent. A person-centred approach is defined by ensuring that individuals receive support in the areas they want it, and, in the way in which they want that support delivered. It is empowering, not disabling, and gives vulnerable people more choice in an environment where traditionally choice has been taken away. My role is to coordinate the care and support of individuals with enduring mental health issues.

One person with a diagnosis of schizophrenia had been in care since the age of 19, first in a psychiatric hospital and then in a care home. Now in her early forties, she was displaying hoarding behaviour alongside the symptoms of schizophrenia. Her room was cluttered and infested with flies and was, staff felt, unlivable. The woman herself, on the other hand, was happy with the current state of affairs, and distrustful of people who wanted to help make the room meet health and safety requirements. Any approach that was too inflexible would cause her to become verbally abusive.

It took time to build a relationship of trust with the staff, and it took even longer for any of us to start helping to declutter the room. The woman reached crisis point when the flies began swarming in a cloud and this was the first step towards letting us in. I learnt from her the importance of giving her control and putting her at the centre of the support, as she eventually built trust with some members of staff.

She didn't want to adopt the logical approach that staff were suggesting, and instead wanted to sporadically choose the items she disposed of. And at the end of the day, who am I, who is anyone, to take that choice away? Perhaps it was due to her schizophrenia that she could not change or see any other approach, but this is what I mean by not supporting the disorder but supporting the individual. You and I know the approaches that either work or do not work for us when we have a task we want to achieve.

The main thing that I have learned through working with this person is that, while a small difference was made in her hoarding behaviour (the hoard became smaller) and the flies did not return, the wider impact is perhaps more important. She started going to the shops alone for the first time in the four years I had worked there; she started drawing money out of her account and handing over her own rent money rather than allowing staff to do it; and she laughed more, engaged more. We may have had a certain way of working, but this individual knew her own way too. She was empowered by staff who relinquished some control and allowed her to make her own choices.

The support worker

Paul provides his insight into his experience so far working in cluttered homes, and the life experiences and skills that are useful and helpful to the role.

I have now been working for about six months with Hoarding Disorders UK as a support worker, and I am loving it. It is such a privilege to walk, or in some cases climb, over the threshold and into someone's life.

You have to love people to do this job and I have had the honour of meeting some very interesting and lovely people, from a veteran of the Second World War to a scientist.

I really was not sure what to expect when I applied for the job, but my 60 years of life experience and all the ups and downs that brings has equipped me quite well. For most of my career I worked in sales and although that was business to business it still involved building a rapport and a good relationship with the person I was dealing with.

I also worked for four years in the inclusion centre of a mainstream secondary school with children who had behavioural, emotional and/or social issues. That experience too has helped me in communicating with the varied mix of people who are hoarders and their families.

During my probation period I read a lot and watched some videos. I shadowed Jo in hoarders' homes and at multi-agency meetings. It was an excellent grounding and has given me the confidence to work on my own with a person or a member of their family.

Building a rapport is the most important thing to do and everyone has a story to tell. By talking and listening to people you get to understand them and their feelings, which is invaluable in how you tackle the job and work together. When you can make a difference to someone's life it is incredibly empowering not just for the person but for you as well. You have to work with people to really see the benefits, and it can be good fun working as a team and tackling the issues and the stuff together.

We have recently been working with a family in which one of the teenage boys has not been engaging, spending the vast majority of the day in his bedroom without talking to anyone. When I spoke to him about working together to tidy his room, he readily agreed. It was not long before we were chatting away, and the work then became effortless and very rewarding.

I have learnt a lot from my colleagues within Hoarding Disorders UK, from others within the different agencies we work with and from other people who work with hoarders.

I have never had a job before that is so rewarding in terms of helping people. It is not always a success – sometimes it does not work because of a family dynamic or a weak link in the multi-agency approach, and that can be tough to take. But you always have to move on quickly and work and help someone else.

Myths and truths

The following list of myths and truths has been compiled by the Chief Fire Officers Association and gives a good illustration of their approach to hoarding. It appears on their website and was used to raise hoarding awareness in 2014.

Myth: Removing clutter and property will remove the issue of hoarding.
Truth: Large scale clean-ups without the person's permission do not work – it is likely to have a long-term negative impact on the person's mental health. Large scale clean-ups even with the person's permission may not work. There are no medications proven to be effective for hoarding yet.

Myth: Fires in hoarding properties will behave in the same way as they do anywhere else.
Truth: Fires were contained to the room of origin in 90 per cent of all residential fires. In hoarding homes, however, that percentage dropped to 40 per cent, indicating that hoarded materials promote the spread of fire through a dwelling.

Myth: Hoarding only takes place in certain types of property.
Truth: Hoarding can be found in all property types and all types of tenure. Hoarding properties in high-rise premises pose very particular risks to the community and to firefighters. Hoarding in private residences creates some specific issues with regards to the application of legislation.

Myth: People with hoarding issues can't see all the stuff and dirt, they don't mind it.
Truth: They can see it but they need to mentally block it out. It is called clutter blindness. But when they do start to talk about it, this can be a sign they are ready for change and help.

Myth: There is nothing we can do about it.
Truth: With the proper support, help and guidance, hoarding problems can be resolved.

Myth: People with hoarding issues love their belongings more than their family.
Truth: They have extended their personality into everything in their

lives and so they will shut down if pushed too much by loved ones to discard things that all have an equal value to them.

Myth: People with hoarding issues are just dirty and lazy.
Truth: Usually just the opposite is true. But they have often undergone a traumatic experience or had a huge period of instability in their lives. They experience shame and fear, which paralyses them and makes it very difficult to understand how they can return to the way they were before. Incorrect intervention can often cause further trauma if they feel they have been perceived to be someone who they are not.

Myth: People with a tendency to hoard are lazy, dirty people who like living in cluttered environments.
Truth: Individuals with a tendency to hoard are not gender or societal specific. Many things can contribute to this complex condition, including biological, psychological and social factors.

Myth: All people with hoarding issues have OCD.
Truth: OCD and hoarding disorder are distinct conditions which were once linked when studies first started.

Myth: People only hoard things at home.
Truth: Hoarding in offices and other business premises is not uncommon, and can lead to blocked escape routes and increased risk of a fire.

Myth: Evicting people with hoarding issues teaches them a lesson and stops them hoarding again.
Truth: Being evicted is a traumatic experience, and can create such anxiety for those with hoarding issues that their tendency to hoard can increase.

Myth: People with hoarding issues don't like to talk about it.
Truth: There are currently various support groups around the UK, mainly in London.

Myth: All people with hoarding issues live in squalid conditions or own numerous pets, or both.
Truth: Not all people with hoarding issues live in unhygienic conditions, or are animal hoarders.

Myth: Every room in a hoarder's home is packed full of stuff.

Truth: People with less extreme hoarding issues may have parts of their home which are less cluttered, or live with people who aren't hoarders and who do what they can to keep parts of a home tidy.

Myth: People with hoarding tendencies are uneducated and have lower levels of intelligence.
Truth: Individuals with hoarding tendencies are often intelligent and highly educated.

Myth: Hoarding is a 'lifestyle choice'.
Truth: In May 2013, hoarding disorder was reclassified as a condition in its own right under the US *Diagnostic and Statistical Manual of Mental Disorders* V (DSM-V) (American Psychiatric Association, 2013). The NHS generally uses the World Health Organization's International Classification of Diseases (ICD-10) system to diagnose mental health conditions rather than the US DSM-V. Hoarding disorder is not yet included in ICD-10 but this is currently being considered.

Myth: Hoarding is caused by a traumatic life event.
Truth: It's not clear what causes hoarding, therefore it is important not to assume that a traumatic life event is the reason behind an individual's hoarding behaviour – there could be a number of contributory factors and events. It is far more likely to affect those with a family history of hoarding; genetics and upbringing are likely to be among the contributing factors.

Myth: Everyone with lots of clutter is a hoarder.
Truth: Just because someone owns lots of stuff or lives in a cluttered home, doesn't necessarily mean they're a hoarder.

10

The voice of the hoarder

As this book aims to illustrate, hoarding is a complex, multi-faceted issue. Sometimes I think it wouldn't be going too far to say that there are as many types of hoarders as there are individuals! Although this book can't cover every type of hoarding experience, this chapter features a selection of people's own experience of hoarding, with stories from hoarders who have reclaimed their space.

K's story

K's is a very powerful story and indicates the determination and strength a person can draw from a support network. After years of surrounding himself with stuff which acted as a wall preventing people from getting too close or allowing himself to be hurt, K ultimately turned his life around to allow people to act as his support system.

I am pleased that Heather Matuozzo from Clouds End is sharing K's story with us and we do hope this provides inspiration for others. Heather founded the first social enterprise dedicated to working with people with hoarding issues, training in hoarding awareness and raising awareness wherever possible. Heather had two aunts who were hoarders, one of whom was her favourite. She stayed at her aunt's house every weekend as a child and loved it: 'It was like waking up in a treasure trove.'

So when she was working as a professional organizer and was contacted by a national children's charity who asked her to work with a lady whose children had been taken away from a hoarded home, she jumped at the chance. This opened a door to a need that was not being met anywhere in the UK at the time. It was around 2007, when local authorities had no strategies in place for working with people with hoarding issues. So Clouds End was born . . .

Heather developed the first training course in hoarding awareness and is now the foremost trainer in the UK.

Through Clouds End, Heather works with many local authorities up and down the UK. She uses her one-to-one experiences to illustrate how to work with people who hoard. She has been a consultant to the BBC and appeared in two series of *Britain's Biggest Hoarders*, and she often talks on the radio. She runs three support groups in Solihull and Birmingham and has developed a book to use with support groups. Clouds End CIC sponsors the resource websites <www.nationalhoardingtaskforce.co.uk> and <www.hoardingawarenessweek.org.uk>.

The most powerful voice is the voice of the person. That voice knows all there is to know. Hear that voice, listen to what it asks for, feed that information back to help create and develop strategies and plans and then finally use that voice to help others.

I know a man called K.

He describes in his own words how he has always tried to hide behind things to keep himself safe. First, as a child, he said he built a wall with his belongings – but as he was just a child those weren't allowed to stay up long.

As an adult he took to alcohol. He said he needed to keep people away from him, so drinking did that – until he stopped many years ago.

Then he started to hoard possessions and also to neglect his self-care. His house got so bad he asked his friends (of whom he has a good network) to come in and clear it with him, which they did. But then he felt so bad, so bereft and lost that it affected him badly. He could no longer turn to his friends for help. He was so confused and desolate, he filled his home again faster and ended up living mainly in his hall. He was talking to a friend one day about how he had found a good yoga mat in a skip and was going to use it as a bed on top of the stuff in his hall. His friend burst into tears and said she hated to think of him living like that. She mentioned that she had seen an advert for a local hoarding support group. K joined – he said he was delighted to meet like-minded people and was struck by everyone's support and goodwill towards him.

He had a good think about his home and decided that he really wanted to tackle his situation. He knew that he didn't want anyone to be in there with him, he felt he needed to process his stuff himself. But he did like the idea of someone knowing that he was working. So he would text his friend that he was starting and she would text him back half an hour later.

That was how he worked through his home. Just half an hour a day, but he stuck to it. He said he realized as he was going through things that he was actually depressed, and so he sought help for that. He hadn't realized that he had buried everything – layers of unhappiness –.in those piles. He said it was very painful going through it all but cathartic, and he made it. His home is now clear and has stayed clear for a long time.

K has primed all his friends to keep an eye on him. They know if they spot things building up that they can bring it to his attention. He lost a close relative recently, and realizing this might be a trigger, he asked his friends to keep a closer eye on him. But he got through that experience, not without pain, but without it affecting his living conditions. He did say he has a new problem now . . . he needs to decorate and doesn't know where to start!

K has shared his story and uses his experiences to help others. He speaks straight from the heart, with a powerful voice.

Child of a hoarder

Cherry Rudge, founder of Rainbow Red, a team of professional declutterers, is herself the daughter of a hoarder, so she has experienced the day-to-day physical, psychological and emotional challenges faced by families affected by living with too much stuff, and the extreme sensitivities required to calmly help people declutter and create order out of chaos. This is Cherry's story and as relevant as all the other stories in this book, but it is particularly pertinent in that she is now one of the leading hoarding specialists in the UK. Cherry became the Marketing, PR & Partnerships Officer of The Association of Professional Declutterers & Organizers UK (APDO) in 2011, and has been pioneering and campaigning ever since. She is also a member of the Chief Fire Officers Association's Hoarding Working Group.

As a child and a teenager, I never really thought of my dad as a hoarder – it wasn't a term that was ever used around the house. It's only since my mum died in 2009 and I started helping an elderly lady bring order to her cluttered, chaotic home that it occurred to me that it was a familiar environment to me (so not at all daunting), and that I'd been brought up in a hoarder's home.

Dad never understood why we got so annoyed about the mounds of newspaper clippings, or the various cars, televisions, radios, lawnmowers and motorbikes – or why having a defunct boiler and rubble in the middle of the lawn, or unfinished DIY/property maintenance, or inaccessible parts of the house was a problem, or unattractive and unnecessary.

While I found Dad's accumulated stuff and eccentric behaviour very embarrassing, I think my brother rather enjoyed being surrounded by boys' toys! It was utterly frustrating for my mum though; she said drawing and painting was her way of meditating and temporarily escaping from the areas of chaos that she wasn't allowed to keep clean and tidy.

Here's a brief summary of my dad's story. As you'll see, he had very little control over what happened to him during the early years of his life, which I believe probably resulted in him over-compensating as he got older so that he had control over his 'comfort zone'.

My dad was an only child, born in 1930. His parents weren't the affectionate or encouraging type (he didn't turn out to be either), and he was brought up by elderly aunts with an old-fashioned Victorian attitude, uncaring towards children. For example, from the age of only eight he was regularly put on a train in London by himself to visit relatives in North Wales – something that would be frowned upon today. Later he was evacuated to Devon during the war. Conscription to National Service meant he had very little control over his late teens and early twenties either.

The end of wartime rationing in 1954 meant that once things became available, Dad became an avid early adopter of anything related to technology, computers or engineering. He moved to a Surrey commuter-belt village within a couple of years of getting married – presumably to escape his childhood memories of war-torn London and live in the countryside that he loved. He became king of his castle – his comfort zone – for more than 50 years.

When his neighbour moved house he bought the other half of the semi-detached property, and converted it into one house by himself. His possessions expanded to fit the space, with shed begetting shed, and television sets seeming to breed and spread around the house like Tribbles. There were two staircases, only one of which could be navigated due to the accumulation of stuff. There would inevitably be one car in use and another available for spares. At its peak we probably had about seven vehicles parked in the drive, including one of mine and one of my brother's. Dad did all the car servicing himself, but he would never get rid of things like empty oil cans, which either became drawers or containers for something in his garage, or accumulated in a pile outside – along with all sorts of other detritus.

The more I've researched hoarding, the more I've come to realize my dad was also probably on the autism spectrum, as he showed classic symptoms from all three areas of the triad of impairments: impairment of imagination, impairment of social communication, and impairment of social relationships.

The only time that organizing and clearing some of the clutter from his home really became possible to any great extent was towards the end of his life, after Mum had died, when he was diagnosed with dementia which rapidly became worse. It took me the best part of two years (on and off, between working and being his primary carer) to organize his paperwork, bringing together piles in disintegrating carrier bags from all over the house, so that I could eventually manage his affairs once lasting power of attorney was in place. Thank goodness I found a brilliant member of Solicitors for the Elderly to help us – they've since been excellent with probate too.

Clearing the house so that it could be demolished after Dad died took over a year. Ironically, despite the subsidence, had regular maintenance been done every five years or so, the cracks wouldn't have been as bad and it probably wouldn't have had to be knocked down.

Hey ho – maybe he knew he could never make it perfect, so he didn't try . . .

Brian's story

Here is an overview from a gentleman with whom we have been working for just over a year – approximately 216 hours. The work was done at a pace suitable to him but which may or may not suit anyone else, as Brian is 84 years old. Brian has now regained his home, and his family were able to come for Christmas dinner and sit at the dining table in 2015 for the first time in 15 years.

First, a bit of history. When I left school in 1948 aged 16 I had been building my own wireless sets for a number of years. At that time there was a plethora of government surplus radio and radar equipment available at ridiculously low prices. I am not sure whether the term electronics was widely used; it was several decades later when the magazine *Wireless World* was renamed *Electronics World*. Suffice it to say that I spent my spare cash buying assorted electronic items, including items such as British and American Bomb Sight computers. It was rumoured that the dealers were purchasing surplus at £50 per lorryload, and it was easy to amass a varied assortment of radio and radar receivers. I still have a radar chassis (price seven shillings and sixpence or 37.5p), which was six feet high laid on its side – it forms a substantial bench for my lathe. I also have a large and enticing assortment of electronic items which formed the basis of my garage clutter.

Fast forward to the late 1990s. The clutter had spread throughout our house and my son advised me to stop buying 'stuff'. Sadly, I ignored the advice and continued to collect 'bargains' including many items of computer equipment, together with furniture, electrical equipment, lighting, DIY items and many DIY and computer magazines. I take great pleasure in lighting, lampshades, the way the light reflects off glass, dimmers, LED lighting and anything that captures rainbows of colours. I love anything that twinkles and almost anything that has a plug on it. I take great delight in tools and gadgets – anything that measures time and heat. My family tease me for taking the latest catalogues from Screwfix and Toolmaster to read in bed.

I retired in 1993 but my wife continued working until 1999, when she was made redundant after a misunderstanding with her manager. She subsequently developed Alzheimer's disease. With the benefit of hindsight, I believe her dementia began that year. We were fortunate that she was always happy, never nasty or dirty. Every day she asked 'Are we going out?' and we would go to a garden centre for coffee and cake, and would buy a plant or tree which we neither needed nor had room for. This is not to assign blame to my wife for the clutter in the garden, but our frequent trips out did result in a plethora of 'stuff' bought at the garden centres as part of our excursions together. I accept full responsibility for the purchases. Once a week we would also visit a City market and would return with several carriers of clutter.

I maintained safe movement throughout the house and fitted an additional handrail on the stairs. I also installed a bath hoist because it was difficult to help a soapy, slippery lady out of the bath. Our shower cubicle was small and inconvenient. I purchased a large walk-in shower unit but did not get around to fitting it, so it became another item of clutter in the doorway to the spare bedroom, which was already full. I had many plans for projects but with the lack of space I was unable to follow through with them.

In 2011 I employed a local care agency to help me declutter. Unfortunately, the help they sent consisted of a university vacation student and her young sister, a school leaver. The task was beyond their capability and culminated in me having to search through six bin bags to find my power of attorney, bank statements and income tax papers. I had asked them to tidy the top of the piano but they had carried on to empty an adjacent box. Fortunately I noticed that the box was missing when my wife and I returned from our trip out. This highlights the need to seek advice from competent authorities such as social services and to be cautious about whose support you are seeking.

My wife went into a care home 20 miles away in late August weighing only six stone, and she passed away just before Christmas. It had been a 24/7 job caring and visiting, one which I undertook quite happily, but I did not then have the motivation to start decluttering.

Two and a half years later I was admitted to hospital for heart surgery. Upon my return home, a friend came to see me and said that she had been in touch with social services, who visited me and suggested that they could recommend a company who could assist me with decluttering the house. Without a doubt this was the best thing that had happened to me for a number of years. It was the start of my journey back from deepest clutter land. My home had become much more cluttered and I was having to step over carrier bags on the floor of the lounge!

The declutterers from HD UK visited me and I was very pleased to note that I was dealing with experienced, competent people. There have been occasions when I have regretted letting items go but some have been returned the following week. There have been quite a few occasions when I have been unsure whether to let things go. They suggested asking me the following week and we agreed to create a category of 'keep for a week', although I have on occasion stretched it to several weeks. We have established a friendly atmosphere, such that I look forward to their visits even if it does sometimes mean parting with familiar items. All the items removed are meticulously recorded on an individual form each week.

The process is not cheap but the costs relate to my willingness to quickly dispose of surplus or redundant items. When I commented to my daughter that I was putting value into my home, she quickly responded by pointing out how much it is improving the quality of my life. I cannot disagree; it is pleasant to respond to the doorbell without worrying what to say if someone needs to come in.

When a house becomes badly cluttered the occupant regards it as a normal state and becomes 'clutter blind'. The same comment applies to overhead cobwebs! My home is now a much nicer place to be and the coastline of 'normality' is coming quite near.

Finally, I would like to express my gratitude to the instigators and implementers of the process of regaining all the lost space in my home. My house is now my home again and I am no longer embarrassed about asking people in. My daughter and her family were able to enjoy Christmas lunch with me last year in the dining room that I am now reunited with, and even to stay in my spare room, which had been used as a storage unit for my stuff. My before and after photos act as a real prompt and reminder of where I was and how much better life feels now. I have now managed to employ a cleaner: there are surfaces to be cleaned, floors to be washed, and clear carpet to vacuum.

Finally, I'd like to include another list of myths and truths, this time taken directly from members of the hoarding support groups I run in Newbury and Bracknell. I believe these will help reduce the stigma around hoarding, and help raise awareness of hoarding for those that know very little about it.

Myth: Hoarder is another term for collector.
Truth: Collections are usually a well-organized, clear set of items. Hoarding may be a collection of items, but this may not be clear or well organized, and it will be detrimental to the person's living space.

Myth: You can go in and clear out all of the clutter and that will help the person to keep it that way.
Truth: No – this approach will usually lead to trauma for the person concerned, and a greater problem which is very quickly built up again, sometimes to a greater degree than previously.

Myth: I just need more space.
Truth: No amount of space will help if the underlying problem is not addressed.

Myth: Hoarders can't stop hoarding.
Truth: With help and support and the correct treatment, people can overcome their hoarding behaviours and rid themselves of items they no longer want or need.

Useful addresses

This section includes resources, organizations and assistance that can help nationally in the UK, as well as useful websites and forums for hoarders and their friends and families.

General

British Association for Behavioural & Cognitive Psychotherapies
Imperial House
Hornby Street
Bury
Lancashire BL9 5BN
Tel.: 0161 705 4304
Website: www.babcp.com

British Psychological Society
St Andrews House
48 Princess Road East
Leicester LE1 7DR
Tel.: 0116 254 9568
Website: http://beta.bps.org.uk

Chief Fire Officers Association (CFOA)
Free 'Safe and Well' visits are available.
Website: www.cfoa.org.uk

For facts and figures on hoarding:
www.cfoa.org.uk/17652

Cruse Bereavement Care
PO Box 800
Richmond
Surrey TW9 1RG
National Helpline: 0808 808 1677
Website: www.cruse.org.uk

London Fire Brigade
To book a safety visit:
www.london-fire.gov.uk/HomeFireSafetyVisit.asp
Or call 0800 028 44 28

OCD Action
506–507 Davina House
137–149 Goswell Road

London EC1V 7ET
Tel.: 0845 390 6232
Website: www.ocdaction.org.uk

Hoarding websites

Help for Hoarders
Advice, support and forum run by Jasmine Harman:
www.helpforhoarders.co.uk

www.compulsive-hoarding.org
www.compulsive-hoarding.org/Test.html (test yourself for compulsive hoarding)
www.counselling-directory.org.uk/compulsive-hoarding.html
www.flylady.net
www.hoardingdisordersuk.org
www.hoardinguk.org (for phone, email and advocacy support free of charge)
http://life-pod.co.uk
www.nhs.uk/Conditions/hoarding/Pages/Introduction.aspx (NHS page on hoarding disorder)
www.ocduk.org/hoarding

Professional declutterers

Association of Professional Declutterers and Organisers (APDO)
Fourwinds House
Balderton
Chester CH4 9LF
Website: www.apdo.co.uk

Clouds End CIC
Help for individual hoarders, social services, housing associations, landlords and Primary Care Trusts. Based in Solihull, West Midlands.
Tel.: 0121 680 5287
Website: www.cloudsend.org.uk

Rainbow Red Professional Decluttering, Organising and Project Management
Tel.: 07931 303310 (phone or text)
Website: www.rainbowred.co.uk

Your Living Room CIC
Correspondence to:
The Black Barn
The Folley
Layer-de-la-Haye CO2 0HZ
Tel.: 05600 023662
Website: www.yourlivingroomcic.co.uk

Junk collection and recycling

Contact your local council for details of local recycling and collection facilities. The following charities offer free collection of some items:

British Heart Foundation
Tel.: 0808 250 0030
Website: https://www.bhf.org.uk/shop/donating-goods/
book-a-free-furniture-collection

Emmaus UK (homelessness charity)
Website: www.emmaus.org.uk/shop/donate_goods
Or call in at your local shop.

Sue Ryder
Tel.: 03330 031 883
Website: www.sueryder.org/shop-with-us/donate-to-our-shops/furniture

Other useful websites

Depop (a mobile social shopping app)
www.depop.com

Ebay (well known as an online sales outlet)
www.ebay.co.uk

Freecycle (an online non-profit community for people to give and get stuff free, moderated by local volunteers)
www.freecycle.org

Gumtree (a site for advertising goods for sale or for free)
https://www.gumtree.com

Music Magpie (can help to sell CDs, DVDs, books, games, phones and so on)
www.musicmagpie.co.uk

Stuff U Sell (sell items on your behalf)
www.stuffusell.co.uk (a company that sells items on your behalf)

We Buy Books (helps to dispose of books, CDs, DVDs and games)
www.webuybooks.co.uk

Therapies

Don't forget that the NHS advises that your GP should be the first port of call.

Cognitive behavioural therapy (CBT)
Website: www.cbtregisteruk.com

EMDR (Eye Movement Desensitisation and Reprocessing)

Website: www.emdrassociation.org.uk

EFT (Emotional Freedom Technique or tapping)
Find certified practitioners in the UK at:
www.aametinternational.org
www.eftuniverse.com
You can also visit:
www.thetappingsolution.com

Other sources of help

To find counsellors or psychotherapists who deal with hoarding:
www.counselling-directory.org.uk/compulsive-hoarding.html

Hoarding support groups – some local groups and other resources at:
www.helpforhoarders.co.uk/resources

Further reading

Sheila Chandra, *Banish Clutter Forever: How the Toothbrush Principle Will Change Your Life*, London: Vermilion, 2010.

Randy Frost and Gail Steketee, *Stuff: Compulsive Hoarding and the Meaning of Things*, Boston: Houghton Mifflin 2011.

Alexander Haynes, *Hoarding: Help for Families*, Life Psychology Series, 2015 (Kindle).

Claudia Kalb, *Andy Warhol was a Hoarder: Inside the Minds of History's Great Personalities*, Washington, DC: National Geographic, 2016.

Satwant Singh, Margaret Hooper and Colin Jones, *Overcoming Hoarding: A Self-Help Guide Using Cognitive Behavioural Techniques*, London: Robinson, 2015.

David Tolin, Randy Frost and Gail Steketee, *Buried in Treasures: Help For Compulsive Acquiring, Saving, And Hoarding (Treatments That Work)*, New York: Oxford University Press, 2013.

Index

Hoarding Disorders UK Community Interest Company

Company Number: 8835291

Hoarding Disorders UK is a not for profit Community Interest Company. Our aim is to provide practical hands-on support and expert advice to those affected by the varying levels of hoarding disorder, ranging from the chronically disorganized to extreme hoarders. We support both individuals and their families throughout this process, helping them to reconnect both as a family unit and with the wider local community.

We use a responsible and unique person-centred approach that incorporates professional decluttering, life skills and home organizational skills. We provide an ethical, sustainable and quality approach throughout our work which includes the use of our 8-Step Plan, support groups, research, consultancy, education and training.

We also work collaboratively with other professionals and organizations who are in contact with these individuals and their families.